Understand the Bible

The Biblical Metanarrative Approach

David P. Teague

Other books by Dr. David Teague

Available through Amazon.com and other distributors

GODLY SERVANTS:
Discipleship and Spiritual Formation for Missionaries

THE MISSIONARY CALL:
Seven Aspects of Discernment

SERMONS FOR LENT AND EASTER

UNDERSTAND THE BIBLE: The Biblical Metanarrative Approach
Copyright © 2016 David P. Teague
All rights reserved.
ISBN-13: 978-1533533296
ISBN-10: 1533533296

Written and published for Trinity Discipleship Ministries
trinity.discipleship@gmail.com

Contents

1 The Grand Plan of Scripture

How do we make sense of the Bible? There are 1,189 chapters in the Bible—full of stories, histories, songs and proverbs; crazed kings and heart-broken prophets and abundant displays of human weakness. It can be so perplexing that many people who try to read the Bible give up in confusion. What's it all about? Who can grasp what the Bible is saying as a whole?

Yet there is a grand plan and purpose of God in the Bible. The Apostle Paul calls it, "a plan for the fullness of time" (Ephesians 1:10). Once we grasp this plan, we are much more able to understand the Bible as a whole. That's what this book is about.

What is a Metanarrative?

Some Bible scholars describe God's plan as the *biblical metanarrative*. That may sound like a mouthful, but it really is a very helpful phrase, as we will show. But what is a metanarrative?

Think of it this way…

If you were to read Tolstoy's massive novel *War and Peace* and someone asked you, "What's it about?" there are several answers you could give. You could say it's a rather confusing novel full of romances and ballrooms and an endless procession of difficult names. Or, thinking deeper, you might say that it is about the Napoleonic Wars. Or, thinking still deeper, you might mention what Tolstoy was trying to say about life and war through the many individual stories he told in his novel.

Similarly, at first glance the Bible appears to be just a confusing collection of random stories and sayings. But when we think deeper about the Bible, a unity begins to appear. What is God saying through all the stories, teachings and events recorded?

This is where the word *metanarrative* comes into play. Literary people define a metanarrative as a story that explains other stories. It's the master story that helps everything to make sense. And so, in the movies, for instance, the metanarrative would be the important background story that explains why everything else is happening.

Does the Bible have a metanarrative, a master story? If it does, this would be the key to understanding the Bible as a whole. If we could understand the grand plan and purpose of God, we could make sense of the Bible's different stories and elements.

The many stories and elements of the Bible do seem, at first glance, unrelated and confusing. But when we begin thinking of the Bible in a metanarrative way we start to see unifying themes such as the love of God, the holiness of God and the redemptive purpose of God, to name a few. And we begin noticing that braiding these many strands together there is one thing always happening, namely, that God is constantly revealing and disclosing himself to the world for its redemption. Moreover, we begin noticing that this self-revelation of God always happens in the covenant walk that God has with a people he has chosen.

So, if someone were to ask you, "What's the Bible all about?" you might answer, "It's a mash of ancient stories." Or, thinking in a metanarrative way, you might say, "The Bible speaks of the self-revelation of God through a chosen people for the redemption of the world."

Why is This Important?

This is important because the word *metanarrative* is also being used in another way today—in philosophy, and with major implications for Christianity. In philosophy, a metanarrative is a master story which explains all other stories—all of history, all knowledge and everyone's individual stories and experiences. A perfect example would be Marxism with its all-encompassing explanation of history and human existence.

Christianity is also often regarded as being a metanarrative, a comprehensive explanation of life. For sure, Christianity is based on God's truth, so it is not strictly a modern metanarrative like Marxism which is based on human reasoning. Still, it is regarded as a metanarrative since it is a comprehensive explanation of why everything is the way it is.

But we now live in 'postmodern' times when people are increasingly skeptical about other people's grand explanations of life. As Jean-François Lyotard (1924-1998), a leading philosopher, once said: "Simplifying to the extreme, I define postmodern as incredulity towards metanarratives." Today, people want to feel that they create their own meaning as we each live out our own 'little story.' This is why Christians who talk about their faith to others today will often be told, "That may suit you but my own beliefs work just as well for me."

The postmodern age in which we live says that there are no universal metanarratives that you or I can create. But let's consider the implications of that thought for a moment …

If it is true that there are no universal metanarratives that you or I can create then the only true metanarrative would have to come from God—the ground of our being. And if this is so, then the biblical metanarrative—the plan and purpose of God that explains the many stories in the Bible—becomes very important. Knowing God's purpose for the world as found in the Bible helps us to understand life itself.

This may explain why—as contradictory as it may seem—when people study the Bible today in a metanarrative way, it often resonates deeply within them. Despite our postmodern world, people are still searching for something bigger than themselves to help their lives make sense. When they discover God's plan and purpose, it resounds in their souls.

An example is seen in the story of Kimberly Shumate, who had been involved in the occult. Concerning one particularly poignant moment in her long journey to Christ, she writes of the power of the biblical metanarrative in her life—

> *As Lisa drove me home, my mind ached as I replayed Scott's words. All the Old Testament and New Testament verses had one oddly familiar voice—one tone, one heart. I wondered, "How could a book written by so many different people over the course of hundreds of years fit together perfectly as if one amazing storyteller has written the whole thing?" The Holy Spirit began melting my vanity and arrogance with a power stronger than any hex, incantation, or spell I'd ever used. Suddenly, the blindfold I'd worn for almost 30 years was stripped away, and instantly I knew what I'd been searching for: Jesus!*

From <u>Today's Christian Woman</u>, Vol 24, No 5 (2002).

Is There Really a Biblical Metanarrative?

Many people today doubt that the Bible is anything more than just an old collection of stories and sayings. Some say that the Scriptures are 'a multi-voiced tapestry' that can be interpreted in 'myriads of ways.' They see no unity at all in the Bible. At most, they say, the Bible just reports the experiences of different people with God with no real direction to it other than that. There is no metanarrative, no master story and no grand plan which unites all the particular stories of the Bible.

We see things differently: that the Bible speaks of the self-revelation of God to the world for its redemption—a self-revelation that reached its culmination in the Incarnation, when the "Word became flesh" (John 1:14). As F. F. Bruce once wrote in his classic book, *The New Testament Documents: Are They Reliable?* —

... the Christian gospel ... tells how for the world's redemption God entered into history, the eternal came into time, the kingdom of heaven invaded the realm of earth, in the great events of the incarnation, crucifixion, and resurrection of Jesus the Christ.

Or, to put it another way, *if there was an Incarnation, then there is a biblical metanarrative*. The Incarnation did not just happen one day as a casual event; rather, it took place in the greater context of God's self-revelation to the world. That context is the biblical metanarrative. The many stories and sayings of the Bible are not simply records of unrelated things, but they all relate to the Incarnation and its purpose in some way.

Did the Church Invent the Biblical Metanarrative?

Some argue that the Church invented the biblical metanarrative and that the New Testament fulfills the Old only in the sense of imposing its own story on it.

But this accusation is hardly justified. It ignores the obvious "order and the connection of the Scriptures," in the words of the second-century theologian Irenaeus. He was dealing with a dangerous heresy known as Gnosticism, which distorted the order and connection of Scripture. Irenaeus says of them—

Their manner of acting is just as if one, when a beautiful image of a king has been constructed by some skillful artist out of precious jewels, should then take this likeness of the man all to pieces, should rearrange the gems, and so fit them together as to make them into the form of a dog or of a fox, and even that but poorly executed; and should then maintain and declare that this was the beautiful image of the king which the skillful artist constructed. (Against Heresies, 8)

The objection that the Church invented the biblical metanarrative also ignores the reality of the Incarnation. As stated before, if there was an Incarnation, then there has to be a biblical metanarrative. The Incarnation was such a climactic event that the faithful naturally began to read the Old Testament in its light. We do the same with any story. During the telling, we're not quite sure how the story all fits together. We begin to fully understand the plan and plot of a story only when we reach its culmination, that is, its fulfillment.

To understand the concept of the _fulfillment_ of Scripture, it is helpful to think of the word _emergence_ as used in the natural sciences. Emergence is the name given for new and unforeseen properties that emerge as simpler structures become more complex. For instance, a hurricane is an emergent phenomenon. It is a highly organized system that arises from the interaction of its simpler components of heat and water vapor. The structure of a hurricane is latent within these simpler components but that structure remains hidden until the hurricane develops. In the same way, God's plan of redemption was not fully understood by the faithful in the time of the Old Testament until the "fullness of time" arrived. Only then did the faithful comprehend God's plan and clearly see its presence in the Old Testament. In this way Christ fulfills the Old Testament.

Jesus clearly understood himself to be that culmination to God's plan. In Mark 1:15 he announced, "The time is fulfilled, and the kingdom of God is at hand; repent and believe in the gospel." In making this statement, Jesus is claiming that God had a plan to usher in a kingdom, and that he, Jesus, is the fulfillment of that plan as the Messiah. This is why he saw himself in the Old Testament, written hundreds of years before his time—

> _"And beginning with Moses and all the Prophets, he interpreted to them in all the Scriptures the things concerning himself" (Luke 24:27)._

The Apostle Paul also believed in the plan of God. In Ephesians 3:10 he calls it _'oikonomia,'_ which means 'plan' in Greek but with a connotation of God's managerial intentions for the world—"a plan for the fullness of time." Paul says that the mystery behind God purposes is now finally cleared up: with the Incarnation, God now wants salvation to come to all peoples and not just to the Jews (Ephesians 1:9-12, 3:3-4, 3:8-9, 6:19, Romans 16:25-26, Colossians 1:25-27). Paul prays for the Gentiles in the Ephesian church to be able to grasp the significance of this (Ephesians 3:14-21). And he interprets his own apostleship as important in its fulfillment (Ephesians 3:1-13).

In addition to Jesus and Paul, the first Christians also believed in the grand plan of God. They saw some biblical passages as openly predicting the Messiah, such as when Micah 5:2 says that the Messiah would be born in Bethlehem, or when Isaiah 7-9 speaks of a child named Immanuel, *'God with us,'* or when Isaiah 53 says there would be a Suffering Servant who dies an atoning death.

But they also began to draw illustrative parallels between the Old Testament and the New in the light of the coming of Christ. Bible scholars call these dot-to-dot connections, *type-and-antitype.* Here, the word 'type' is the original image in the Old Testament which is fulfilled in some way by the 'antitype' in the New.

An example would be the Temple. As a physical dwelling place for God in the midst of Israel, the Temple is a symbol of the Incarnation when, "The Word became flesh and dwelt among us" (John 1:14). This association between the Temple and the Incarnation is not arbitrary but is consistent with God's intent, seen from the Garden of Eden, to dwell among his people.

This is why Jesus claimed to be the antitype fulfillment of the Temple when he said—

> *"Destroy this temple, and in three days I will raise it up." 20 The Jews then said, "It has taken forty-six years to build this temple, and will you raise it up in three days?" 21 But he was speaking about the temple of his body. (John 2:19-21)*

Another example of a type-and-antitype fulfillment is when Jeremiah preached about Rachel weeping for her children. In doing so, Jeremiah was most certainly talking about the horror felt by Judean mothers whose children had died because of the exile (Jeremiah 31:15). But Matthew 2:17-18 says these words were *fulfilled* in the Christ story, when Herod slaughtered the children of Bethlehem. What's going on here?

Here, Matthew '*fulfilled*' Jeremiah's prophecy in the sense of using Jeremiah's emotion-packed words to express Bethlehem's horror. In a similar way, when Adam Lanza shot dead 20 children in 2012 at the Sandy Hook elementary school not far from my home, I also used Jeremiah's words in my sermon to give voice to my congregation's grief.

Type-and-antitype parallels, then, are of two kinds. Some represent a theological theme that emerges into completeness in Christ—such as with the Temple symbolizing the Incarnation. Other parallels simply vivify the Christ story—such as with the example of Rachel weeping for her children. Both have an original historical context which is then completed in some way in the larger redemptive purpose of the Bible.

In this book we'll look at some of the more significant type-and-antitype parallels in which a theological theme of the Old Testament emerges into its fullest development in Christ.

How Has God's Plan Been Described?

The name used for the study of individual texts and themes in the Bible in relation to the progressive self-revelation of God as a whole is *biblical theology.*

Below are nine different approaches in biblical theology that have been used through the centuries to describe the plan of God in the Bible. We should keep in mind, though, that any attempt to organize or summarize the entirety of the Bible will have its limitations. For this reason, it is perhaps best to regard these various approaches as *metanarrative frameworks*: that is, they are attempts to portray the plan and purpose of God in Scripture but not exhaustively nor necessarily exclusive of other frameworks—

1. The Jewish Two-Age Division of History

An early attempt to describe the plan of God was the *two-age division of history* common in the time of Jesus among those Jews who were waiting for the Messiah. They called the time before the arrival of the Messiah, the 'present age' (Hebrew: *'olam hazeh*), while the age of the Messiah was known as the 'age to come' (Hebrew: *'olam haba*). We see this very clearly in such verses as Mark 10:29-30, Matthew 12:32, Ephesians 1:21 and Hebrews 6:5. For instance, a translation of the Bible known as the *Complete Jewish Bible* renders Mark 10:29-30 as—

> *Yeshua said, "Yes! I tell you that there is no one who has left house, brothers, sisters, mother, father, children or fields, for my sake and for the sake of the Good News, who will not receive a hundred times over, now, in the 'olam hazeh, homes, brothers, sisters, mothers, children and lands — with persecutions! — and in the 'olam haba, eternal life.*

2. The Old and New Covenants

Another way of organizing the plan of God is by *old and new covenants*. It's based on the prophecy of the new covenant in Jeremiah 31 in which God declares—

> *"Behold, the days are coming," declares the LORD, "when I will make a new covenant with the house of Israel and the house of Judah, ³²not like the covenant that I made with their fathers on the day when I took them by the hand to bring them out of the land of Egypt, my covenant that they broke, though I was their husband, declares the LORD. ³³For this is the covenant that I will make with the house of Israel after those days, declares the LORD: I will put my law within them, and I will write it on their hearts. And I will be their God, and they shall be my people."*
> *(Jeremiah 31:31-33)*

Jesus saw his death as instituting this new covenant (Luke 22:20), as did the early Christians (see 2 Corinthians 3:6,14; Galatians 4:24 and Hebrews 8:6-13). By the 2nd century AD, the church was using the term 'old covenant' to refer to Scripture written before the coming of the Messiah, and 'new covenant' for Scripture written after his arrival. Of course, we know this division as the Old and New Testaments, after '*testamentum*,' the Latin translation of the Greek word for covenant, '*diatheke*.'

3. The Plot Sequence: Creation, Fall, Redemption, Restoration

Irenaeus (ca. 125-202 AD) was an early biblical theologian. In his time, Gnosticism was in vogue—the most dangerous heresy of the 2nd century. The Gnostics claimed to possess secret teachings from the Apostles. Irenaeus argued successfully against them by saying that all the churches founded by the Apostles kept to a common 'Rule of Faith' which helped them interpret Scripture. The early Church eventually summed up this 'Rule' in the Apostles' Creed, but it also described the Rule in a plot-sequence summary of the Bible, namely: "Creation, Fall, Redemption, Restoration."

This sequence is still often used today to summarize the Bible. Its weakness is that it jumps from the Fall to Redemption without adequately considering the history of Israel. God revealed himself to the world by walking in covenant with the descendants of Abraham—this, too, is an important part of the biblical metanarrative which should not be overlooked.

4. Covenant Theology

In the 16th and 17th centuries, Reformed theologians described the biblical metanarrative in terms of the covenants God made with Adam, Noah, Abraham, Moses, David and the New Covenant in Christ. This approach is called *covenant theology*.

Historically, covenant theology has been a very helpful and influential way of understanding the Bible.

5. Dispensationalism

In the 19th century, John Nelson Darby (1800-82) and his followers organized the Bible into 'dispensations,' periods of biblical history. Dispensationalism has had several iterations through the years and is still popular in different circles.

6. History of Redemption

Since the Bible depicts God's self-revelation to the world through a chosen people, the major events within that relationship become a way of understanding the Story of God. The basic plot-line would be: Creation, the Fall, the Call of Abraham, the Exodus, Israel as a Nation, Israel in Exile, the Restoration, and the Fulfillment in the Messiah.

With each of these major events, or epochs, certain aspects of God's character were either revealed or emphasized—

Major Event:	God As:
Creation	Creator
The Fall	Judge
Call of Abraham	Covenant-Maker
Exodus	Redeemer
Israel as a Nation	King
Israel in Exile	The Holy One
The Restoration	The Merciful One
Fulfillment	The Suffering Servant

7. The Thematic Approach

Some biblical theologians depict the biblical metanarrative by tracing one of its major unifying themes, such as the kingdom of God or the mission of God. For examples of this approach, see the recommended reading list in chapter ten.

8. The Worldview Approach

A worldview is an interpretive matrix by which we understand the world. Ravi Zacharias points out that every coherent worldview will answer the following four questions—

Where did I come from?
What is the meaning of life?
How do I define right from wrong?
What happens to me when I die?

"Those are the fulcrum points of our existence," Zacharias says. As will be described in the next chapter, the metanarrative of Bible can be framed within these four worldview questions.

9. The Bible as Drama

We can also understand God's Big Story as a drama. Every drama revolves around a problem to be resolved. In the Bible we see the elements of this drama as: Paradise Given, Paradise Lost, a Restoration Promised and a Restoration Obtained.

Summary of Chapter One

All of these approaches depict the grand plan of Scripture— the biblical metanarrative—from different angles. In the following chapters we will combine many of them to describe the biblical metanarrative anew. In doing so, we will assume that the Bible depicts the self-revelation of God through a chosen people for the redemption of the world, a plan that culminated in the Incarnation.

Our goal is to provide you, the reader, with a quick yet insightful overview so that you may read and teach the Bible with a more informed understanding of the plan and purpose of God.

2 Creation and the Fall

The Apostle John tells us, "God is love" (John 3:16, 1 John 4:6). He made this assertion because Scripture depicts God as loving the world in three great ways:

First, *God created the world*. His Word brought the universe into existence.

Secondly, *God provides for the world*. God did not just create the world and then abandon it but continues to be involved in it by preserving, sustaining and directing the world toward the fulfillment of his ultimate purposes.

Thirdly, *God is redeeming the world from evil*.

The entire biblical worldview rests on this knowledge of God as Creator, Provider and Redeemer. It is why Scripture constantly speaks of God as acting, speaking, revealing, ruling, redeeming and making anew as he fulfills these purposes.

But in saying, "God is love," John is also asserting that God has a relational nature since love exists only as we know and are known. A person who claims to love but never relates to others is hardly believable. Similarly, if God is love, then God must also wish us to know him and to be known by him as Creator, Provider and Redeemer.

The biblical metanarrative rests on this broad foundation of God's love for the world. Because God loves us, God has been making himself known to us. The Story of that self-revelation is the biblical metanarrative. With this in mind, let us trace the biblical metanarrative, beginning with creation.

Genesis 1

The first verse of the Bible is a factual statement that God exists and is the only source of everything. The Bible does not argue these points—it simply presents them as axiomatic assertions—

In the beginning, God created the heavens and the earth. (Genesis 1:1)

Verse 1 appears to function as a 'headline' to introduce the rest of the creation story. Verse 2 then begins that story by taking us to the moment just before creation itself when it says—

The earth was without form and void,
and darkness was over the face of the deep.
And the Spirit of God was hovering over the face of the waters.
(Genesis 1:2)

In saying there was a formless and empty chaos, verse 2 is not implying the existence of some kind of shapeless, chaotic substance before creation. The ancients found it virtually impossible to conceive of absolute nothingness, so the phrase *'without form and void'*—the negation of form and filling—was more understandable to them. The verse is simply telling us that before God created everything, there was nothing.

Following this description of the 'chaos of nothingness' comes the seven days of creation. The seven-day sequence makes it absolutely clear that God alone created the sky and the sea, the land and all the creatures. There can be no pantheon of gods that rules over separate realms of creation, like a sky god and a sea god. And neither can there be gods that resemble animals, since every beast is just a creature of the Lord God. The seven-day sequence of the creation story is a strong affirmation of monotheism, given to strengthen the faith of the Hebrews who were surrounded by polytheistic peoples.

Within the seven-day structure, many have also noticed the existence of another structure: Days 1-3 are in parallel to Days 4-

6. The first set of days describes realms being created while the second set of days describes what fills those realms—

FORMING THE REALMS	FILLING THE REALMS
DAY 1:	**DAY 4:**
Realm of Light	Sun, Moon, Stars
DAY 2:	**DAY 5:**
Realm of Waters Above & Below	Birds and Sea Creatures
DAY 3:	**DAY 6:**
Realm of the Land	Plants, Livestock, Humans

DAY 7: Chaos is vanquished, God reigns

In other words, God creates by vanquishing the formlessness and emptiness of chaos. This stands to reason. If creation is the opposite of the 'chaos of nothingness,' then creation must be God *forming* the realms of nature and then *filling* those realms. By the Seventh Day, God has completed creation: chaos has been formed and filled and God reigns. That is how the story of the Garden in Genesis 2 begins, with our first father and mother living under the reign of God in an unending Seventh Day.

The Foundation of the Biblical Worldview

The account of creation as found in Genesis 1-3 is particularly important because it is the foundation of the entire biblical worldview. A worldview is the overall perspective or matrix by which we understand the world.

Any coherent worldview will provide answers to the following four questions—

1. Where did I come from?
2. What is the meaning of life?
3. How do I define right from wrong?
4. What happens to me when I die?

So, for instance, a person who has a materialistic worldview would assert that: (1) We are no more than a composition of atoms and molecules. (2) There is no meaning to our lives except for the meaning we make. (3) There is no right or wrong except for what we decide. (4) When we die, we revert back to matter and energy without any continuation of the conscious self.

The Genesis creation story provides profoundly different answers to these basic worldview questions—

(1) *"Where did I come from?"* We come from God in whose image we have been created (Genesis 1:26-27).

(2) *"What is the meaning of life?"* We are meant to live in the Seventh Day in God's Garden: abundantly loving and serving God and one another (Genesis 2:15, 2:18-24).

(3) *"How do I define right from wrong?"* The story of the Fall in Genesis 3 answers this question when it describes humanity's search for moral knowledge. It teaches us that true wisdom—the discernment of right from wrong—can only come from knowing God. By itself, our own judgment is imperfect. In the story, the serpent tempts the man and the woman to become "like God, knowing good and evil" (Genesis 3:5)—but only if they act independently of God. When they eat the fruit, they gain a sense of good and evil, but it is a warped moral sense since it comes only from themselves.

This delineates the biblical concept of sin: it is our attempt to be like God without God, which is idolatry of the self. It is living by our own self-centered sense of right and wrong apart from a relationship with God. As a result, sin corrupted the relationship between the man and the woman and caused them to be cast out of the Garden, away from the Presence of God and ending the Seventh Day for them. It also affected their children as we read of Cain killing Abel. Sin also adversely affected God's created world as the violence and wickedness of humanity provoked the

Flood (Genesis 6:5-7). Sin not only mars the human heart, it also scourges creation.

So, in answer to the third worldview question, *"How do I define right from wrong?"* Genesis is saying that sin blights our ability to discern true right from wrong. Only by having our relationship with God restored can we acquire true moral knowledge.

(4) *"What happens to me when I die?"* The short answer from the creation story to the fourth worldview question is, "We will all surely die, but there is also hope."

The fourth worldview question is addressed in Genesis 3:15, when God judges the serpent for deceiving the man and the woman—

> *(Spoken to the serpent)*
> *And I will put enmity*
> *between you and the woman,*
> *and between your offspring and hers;*
> *he will crush your head,*
> *and you will strike his heel. (NIV)*

Previously, God had warned the man and the woman "you will die"—if they ate from the tree. But here, at the time of judgment, God pronounces a death sentence on the serpent when God says, "he will crush your head." The originator of the evil which deceived Adam and Eve will be destroyed by a descendant of Eve, thereby offering hope of a future redemption for humanity.

Some say that this prophecy merely predicts there will be unending conflict between Satan and humanity. But that interpretation turns this pronouncement, which is a word of hope, into a word of despair. It also does not fit in with the rest of Genesis, which speaks of the hope of redemption. This is why traditional interpreters see Genesis 3:15 as prophesying a coming Redeemer, even the Messiah, and they call this verse the *Protevangelium*, or the 'First Gospel.'

The essence of the prophecy centers on the word *'offspring.'* The prophecy speaks of the 'offspring' of the serpent—which apparently are those influenced by the serpent. They hate the offspring of Eve who bear the promise of a champion who will arise from their lineage to strike the serpent a mortal blow, even while the serpent strikes his heel.

So, in answer to the fourth worldview question, "What happens to me when I die?" the creation story asserts that we will indeed die but it then offers us the hope of a Redeemer who will arise to crush the serpent. The rest of the Bible depicts how redemption is accomplished through this Promised Redeemer.

Conflict Arises between the Two Families

God said in Genesis 3:15 that there would be two families in conflict. One apparently would be influenced by the serpent. The other would bear the hope of a Promised Redeemer. We can call this second family, the *Promise Bearers*.

Genesis 4 depicts the outbreak of conflict between these two families. The two sons of Adam and Eve, Abel and Cain, present their offerings to God. Abel's offering is accepted because his heart is right with God. But Cain's offering is rejected because his heart is influenced by evil. He is told, "Sin is crouching at the door. Its desire is for you" (Genesis 4:7). Filled with jealousy against Abel, his brother, Cain rises up and kills him anyways.

The story then lists the descendants of Cain (Genesis 4:17-22) and those of Seth (Genesis 5)—who took the place of Abel, his fallen brother (Genesis 4:25). Subtle contrasts in the genealogies suggest that one family bore the promise of a Redeemer, while the other represents humanity influenced by the serpent. For instance, the seventh in Cain's line from Adam is Lamech, an arrogant, vengeful and violent man (Genesis 4:23-24), while the seventh in Seth's line from Adam is Enoch who "walked with

God" (Genesis 5:24). This contrast between these two individuals seems deliberate, as if Genesis is telling us that each line has ripened until its true nature becomes apparent in the seventh generation.

Also notice how Seth's descendants are said to live to vast ages, but no mention of longevity is given for Cain's descendants. Since longevity was considered to be a sign of divine blessing (compare Exodus 20:12, Deuteronomy 6:2, 32:47), this discrepancy also seems to be a deliberate choice. By mentioning the great ages of Seth's descendants, but not for Cain's line, the account is indicating which family was the 'blessed' line which bore the promise of the coming Redeemer. The long ages may even be hinting at a promise of eternal life through redemption.

The Flood and the Tower of Babel

After the expulsion from the Garden, some of the descendants of Adam and Eve still called on the name of the Lord (Genesis 4:26), but most became corrupt and violent (Genesis 6:11), provoking God to send the Flood to judge their wickedness (Genesis 6-9).

The Flood reminds us of the watery chaos of Genesis 1:2, as if the text is saying that sin promotes chaos. Yet, despite the return of chaos, God mercifully preserves a remnant, revealing God's ultimate intention to bring about human redemption through a descendant of the Promise Bearers. Noah and his family are safe in the Ark, which comes to rest in the receding waters.

Once again, the account purposefully makes a distinction between a 'blessed' family and a family that opposes God. The line of Seth continues in Noah and his son, Shem, from whom came the Semitic peoples (Genesis 10:21-31). The line of Cain had been wiped out by the Flood, but is re-born in the line of the similar-sounding 'Canaan.' Noah curses the line of Canaan for its wickedness, but blesses the line of Shem (Genesis 9:24-27).

The contrast between rebellion and redemption emerges yet once more in Genesis 11 in the story of the Tower of Babel. The tower is an arrogant display of human pride which provokes another outbreak of chaos — this time in the maelstrom of confused human speech (Genesis 11:1-9). Indeed, the word *Babel* sounds like the Hebrew word for '*confused*' in Genesis 11:9.

Yet, despite this outbreak of sin-whipped chaos, chapter 11 ends on a note of hope once again as it lists the names of the Promise Bearers, enumerating them from Shem to Abram (Genesis 11:10-32). And, once again, the longevity of each generation is emphasized *only* for this 'blessed' line, suggesting that this, indeed, is the family that bears the hope of redemption. The list culminates in the call of Abraham in Genesis 12.

Summary of Chapter Two

The creation account of Genesis provides the foundation of the entire biblical worldview. It does so by affirming God's love for the world as Creator, Provider and Redeemer and by answering the four essential worldview questions.

We have traced the lineage of the Promised Redeemer from the First Gospel through the line of Seth until Abraham. In the chapters ahead we will see how the lineage of the Redeemer will descend from Abraham like this—

THE LINEAGE OF THE PROMISED REDEEMER

First Gospel ⇨ Seth ⇨ Abraham ⇨ Israel ⇨ Judah ⇨ David ⇨ The Messiah

3 The Call of Abraham

The book of Genesis is constructed around two major promises. The first is the promise of Genesis 3:15 that a Redeemer would arise from the descendants of Adam and Eve to crush the head of the serpent. The first eleven chapters of Genesis trace the generations that bore this promise of redemption from Seth (Genesis 5:3) to Terah (Genesis 11:32).

The second promise is that given to Abraham, found in Genesis 12:1-3, where his earlier name of Abram is used. It reads:

> Now the LORD said to Abram, "Go from your country and your kindred and your father's house to the land that I will show you. 2 And I will make of you a great nation, and I will bless you and make your name great, so that you will be a blessing. 3 I will bless those who bless you, and him who dishonors you I will curse, and in you all the families of the earth shall be blessed."

These verses are some of the most important in the Bible. In them, notice the repeated use of the word *bless* in its various forms. Especially notice how God tells Abraham, "in you all families of the earth shall be blessed." This blessing is most likely a redemptive blessing, after the manner of the 'First Gospel' of Genesis 3:15, since it is a universal blessing meant for the whole world. This suggests that Abraham and his descendants were chosen to restore, in some way, the lost knowledge of God to the world. Indeed, so ignorant had the world become of God that even Abraham was an idol worshipper when God called him.

The rest of Genesis, chapters 12-50, builds on this promise given to Abraham. In these chapters we see the Chosen People, the family of Abraham, walking with God through four generations. We read of Abraham and Isaac (Genesis 11:27-25:11), Isaac and Jacob (25:19-35:29, 37:1) and Jacob and Joseph (37:2-50:26). The stories are intertwined, generation blurring into generation, as if to say, "Together, we are the Promise Bearers." But let us briefly consider each patriarch separately.

The Abraham Stories (Genesis 12-25)

Abraham is one of the most significant people in history. He was a Bronze Age man who lived over 4000 years ago, yet if historians were to develop a list of the 100 most influential people of all time, Abraham would surely be on that list. The prophet Isaiah said long ago, "Look to the rock from which you were hewn ... look to Abraham your father" (Isaiah 51:1-2). The Apostle Paul says in Galatians 3:29, "And if you are Christ's, then you are Abraham's offspring," meaning we are Abraham's spiritual descendants.

His stories are meant to be our stories. There's a Jewish tradition that says the stories about Abraham teach us how to walk by faith in God. Let's look at the story of Abraham and of all the patriarchs with this in mind.

One thing that immediately strikes us, however, in any honest reading of the patriarchal stories is their open portrayal of human depravity. The stories hide nothing, but freely depict the ugly side of the Chosen Family, the Promise Bearers, in their walk with God.

Twice, Abraham lies about his beautiful wife, Sarah. He fearfully tries to protect himself by identifying her as his sister — an assertion that foolishly places Sarah in danger of rape and causes Abraham to be publicly shamed for his cowardly deception (Genesis 12, 20). If that were not enough, Abraham also convinces himself that it is God's will for him to sleep with Sarah's servant girl (Genesis 16).

We ask, "Why do the stories about Abraham openly display his deficiencies? Why is there no attempt to protect his reputation or to portray him as a hero?" It's true that, later on in the Bible, Abraham is revered as "father" (Isaiah 51:2, Romans 4:16) and called the "friend of God" (James 2:23), but not so in the original stories. There can be only one reason for this blunt honesty in the Abraham Stories: they are not really about Abraham at all, but about God revealing himself to Abraham. Despite Abraham's despicable behavior, God does not give up on him but gradually changes him by grace as Abraham slowly learns to trust in God to be faithful to him.

The stories about Abraham reach their climax when God tells him to sacrifice his son Isaac. After years of walking with God with a faith that was shaky, yet developing, Abraham now perfectly obeys. He has come to trust fully in God's faithfulness as he tells Isaac: "God will provide for himself the lamb for a burnt offering" (Genesis 22:8). Indeed, God does provide a ram in place of Isaac (Genesis 22:13-14), demonstrating not only Abraham's need for atonement but also God's willingness to provide for that need.

The Isaac Stories (Genesis 21-27)

Abraham's presence looms over the stories about his son, Isaac. In fact, the Isaac Stories read simply like a continuation of the Abraham Stories.

We see this clearly in the story of Isaac's birth. Abraham and his wife Sarah were childless, yet God promised to give them an heir. Accordingly, the story of Isaac's birth (chapters 15-18, 21) is told as a story about Abraham's faith in God's promise. The same holds true in the story of the sacrifice of Isaac: its point is to describe the testing of Abraham (Genesis 22). Even Isaac's marriage to Rebekah is depicted as a sign of God's faithfulness to

Abraham (Genesis 23-24). This overlapping seems deliberate, as if to emphasize that Isaac was inheriting Abraham's call and blessing (Genesis 26:2-5, 24; 28:1-4).

The Jacob Stories (Genesis 25-50)

Unlike Isaac, whose stories are completely overshadowed by Abraham, Genesis gives Isaac's son, Jacob, his own spotlight.

Jacob's name in Hebrew means something like "The Trickster." He is a schemer by nature who habitually cheats his way through life. Yet, despite this, he is also a Promise Bearer, an inheritor of the promise given to Abraham and Isaac. And just as God gradually changed Abraham by grace, so we see the same thing happening to the Trickster in the stories about him.

The change in his heart especially begins to become noticeable when he wrestles with the angel at Peniel (Genesis 32). Jacob is about to meet his brother Esau, whom he once had cheated. The night before the encounter, Jacob and his caravan are in the valley of the Jabbok River, down which they had travelled.

Jacob places himself at the rear of the caravan, where he can easily escape alone back up the valley to avoid meeting Esau. However, in the dark, an angel confronts Jacob and wrestles with him until dawn, forcing Jacob to face his brother. When the dreaded meeting finally takes place, Esau is gracious and forgiving toward Jacob instead of harsh and condemning.

This was the beginning of Jacob's redemption, with the angel even changing Jacob's name from *Jacob*, 'The Trickster,' to *Israel*, 'He strives with God.' It was a turning point in his life, but an even deeper healing for him would happen later through the suffering of Jacob's son, Joseph.

The Joseph Stories (Genesis 37-50)

The stories about Joseph occupy fully fourteen chapters, Genesis 37-50, but, oddly, they begin with the words, "This is the account of *Jacob*" (Genesis 37:2, NIV). This is so because the Joseph Stories really are about how Joseph redeemed Jacob.

Jacob had twelve sons—his favorite being Joseph, but Jacob's favoritism sowed the seeds of division within his family. The other sons, torn by jealousy, sold Joseph into slavery, yet God providentially raised Joseph to the heights of power in Egypt. From this position, Joseph enabled Egypt and other surrounding peoples to survive a seven-year famine.

The story of Joseph is told slowly and deliberately to emphasize the providential workings of God. It reaches a dramatic high-point when Joseph meets and then forgives his brothers. His decision to be reconciled to them brings a desperately needed touch of healing to Jacob's troubled family while Joseph's decision to feed them during the famine saves all their lives.

Joseph as a Christ-figure

Joseph is a Christ-figure. He suffers unjustly at the hands of his brothers, yet forgives and feeds them, just as Christ suffered for our sins yet brings us salvation.

Joseph also saved his world. God had promised Abraham that "all the families of the earth" would be blessed through his descendants. Four generations later, Joseph rescues Egypt and its surrounding lands from famine—a partial completion of the promise made to Abraham, which foreshadows a later worldwide fulfillment in Christ.

Although Joseph is a Christ-figure, he is not a direct ancestor of Christ, but only illustrates Christ's character. Genesis 49:10, which has traditionally been regarded as being an early Messianic prophecy, indicates that the Messiah would descend through Joseph's brother, Judah:

> *The scepter shall not depart from Judah,*
> *nor the ruler's staff from between his feet,*

until tribute comes to him;
and to him shall be the obedience of the peoples.

Psalm 78 confirms this promise—saying that God, "rejected the tent of Joseph ... but he chose the tribe of Judah" (Psalm 78:67-68).

Still, because of Joseph's godly character, two traditions about the Messiah grew up among some of the Hebrew people before the time of Jesus. The first tradition described the Messiah as a 'son of Judah' (*bene Yehuda*) who would be a Triumphant King. The other tradition described him as a figurative 'son of Joseph' (*bene Yusef*), who would be a Suffering Servant. Some even speculated that there would be two Messiahs — one to triumph and the other to suffer and die.

In the time of Jesus, most expected that the Messiah would come as a Triumphant King; few thought that he would come as a Suffering Servant. Yet the promise of suffering was present from the very beginning, when Genesis 3:15 warned that the serpent would "strike his heal." It emerges again in the suffering of Joseph and, later, whenever a prophet suffered for speaking in God's name. It reaches a high point in the Old Testament when Isaiah prophesies of a coming Suffering Servant whose death would redeem the people (Isaiah 52:13-53:12).

Jesus identified himself as being this Suffering Servant. We see this from Luke 22:37, when Jesus quotes from Isaiah 53:12 about the Suffering Servant and applies the words to himself:

Luke 22:37
"For I tell you that this Scripture must be fulfilled in me:
'And he was numbered with the transgressors.' For what is written
about me has its fulfillment."

Isaiah 53:12
Therefore I will divide him a portion with the many,
and he shall divide the spoil with the strong,

because he poured out his soul to death
and was numbered with the transgressors;
yet he bore the sin of many,
and makes intercession for the transgressors.

In seeing himself as both the Suffering Servant and the Triumphant King, Jesus combines together in himself the two traditions about the Messiah: Jesus is a 'son of Judah' because he physically descended from Judah through his mother, Mary. But he is also a 'son of Joseph' who would suffer for the sake of others in the tradition of Joseph.

Summary of Chapter Three

As we finish this selective overview of Genesis we can see how it sets the stage for everything that follows. Genesis begins by reminding us that we are meant to be with God, our Creator, in paradise, but the tarnished nature of humanity makes this impossible. Then it shows a merciful God working to restore humanity by promising that a Redeemer would come, a descendant from the line of Eve's Promise Bearers. Abraham and his descendants know themselves to be this Chosen People (Genesis 12:1-3, 17:1-8; 22:16-18; 26:3-5; 26:24; 28:1-4; 35:10-12; 48:3-4). Although they are imperfect, a perfect God is working through them. Genesis ends by dwelling on the Christ-like figure of Joseph who portrays aspects of what the coming Redeemer would be like.

4   The Exodus

Following the call of Abraham, the Exodus became the next major event in the unfolding of God's redemptive plan for the world. After the Israelites went down into Egypt, as described in Genesis, they stayed there for some 400 years. By the time God brought them out, Abraham's once small clan had turned into a nation.

Genesis 15:13-14 tells us that all of this happened to fulfill God's purposes:

> 13 Then the LORD said to Abram, "Know for certain that your offspring will be sojourners in a land that is not theirs and will be servants there, and they will be afflicted for four hundred years. 14 But I will bring judgment on the nation that they serve, and afterward they shall come out with great possessions.

The long stay in Egypt did two things in the lives of the Promise Bearers. First, as mentioned, it enabled them to increase in number. The fertile lands and the comparative safety of Egypt allowed them to multiply until "the land was filled with them" (Exodus 1:7). Secondly, the hardship they endured under the pharaohs made them value their redemption all the more once it happened.

For these reasons, the Exodus became the signature event in Israel's founding as a nation. It shaped her identity, which is why there are over 120 references to the Exodus in the whole Old Testament. It also convinced them that God is a Redeemer, able to rescue them from one of the mightiest of nations. The words, "I am the LORD your God, who brought you out of the land of

Egypt, out of the house of slavery," became seared into the national consciousness (Exodus 20:2).

God Judges Pharaoh and His Gods

There are different opinions about when the Exodus took place. 1 Kings 6:1 says that it happened 480 years before Solomon began construction of the Temple, implying a date around 1446 BC. However, it is possible that this number is symbolic since 480 can represent twelve generations, each lasting forty round years.

The other time period most often considered for the Exodus is during the long reign of Ramesses II, who ruled 1279-1213 BC. He was the greatest and most powerful of all the pharaohs. If the Exodus happened when Egypt was its mightiest, as judgments often do, then Ramesses II would be the man. After him, the marauding '*Sea Peoples*' invaded Egypt, causing it to fall into a centuries-long decline—a weakening that may have begun with God's judgment of Egypt in the Ten Plagues, as recounted in Exodus 7-12.

Whoever the pharaoh of the Exodus was, he would have been ripe for judgment. A pharaoh considered himself to be a son of the god Amun-Ra. He would perform magical rituals to bring order and prosperity to Egypt—supposedly causing the Nile to flow, the sun to shine and the crops to grow. But if a pharaoh's magic ever became weak, the popular belief was that the nation would be engulfed in chaos. This is reflected in such ancient Egyptian texts as '*The Admonitions of Ipuwer*,' written at a different time than the Exodus, but which depicts Egypt awash in national chaos, even saying, "Lo, the river is blood."

This explains why the Ten Plagues took the form they did. The bloody water, the snuffed-out sun and the devastated crops all would be interpreted as signs of the impotence of the pharaoh and his gods. His magic was utterly unable to hold back the chaos. God, who had created the world by bringing order out of chaos, judged Egypt and its gods in the time of Moses by engulfing the nation in chaos once again.

The Passover

The last of the Ten Plagues was the death of all the firstborn in Egypt in the event known as the Passover (Exodus 12). God said:

> *I will strike all the firstborn in the land of Egypt, both man and beast;*
> *and on all the gods of Egypt I will execute judgments: I am the LORD.*
> *(Exodus 12:12)*

This judgment may sound harsh, but we must remember that in the Bible life is a gift from God, not a right; God can withdraw his gift at any time. The Egyptians considered their chief god, Amun-Ra, to be responsible for all life. Striking the firstborn proved the utter inability of Amun-Ra to protect anyone; the tenth plague was a judgment on their chief god.

Moses had instructed the Israelites to mark the outside of their doors with the blood of a lamb to avoid the death of their own firstborn. The first Christians understood the sacrifice of the Passover lambs as pointing to the saving atoning death of Christ. Paul wrote, "Christ, our Passover lamb, has been sacrificed" (1 Corinthians 5:7). Indeed, Jesus shared the Passover meal with the apostles on the day when the Passover lamb was slain (Luke 22:7). That meal, the Last Supper, became the basis for the sacrament of Holy Communion, by which Christians remember their salvation in Christ's atoning death.

Crossing the Sea

As a result of the Passover, the Israelites fled in haste into the desert, only to be pursued by pharaoh and his army. On the shores of the Reed Sea, the Promise Bearers became trapped

(Exodus 14). We read of God providentially sending a strong wind to push back the impassable waters to save them.

The wind is reminiscent of the Spirit of God hovering over the waters of chaos at the beginning of creation. (Wind and spirit are the same word in Hebrew, *'ruach'*—Exodus 14:21, Genesis 1:2). When God leads the Israelites through the waters on dry ground, he is vanquishing the chaos once more to create a nation, just as God had once created the world. But pharaoh's army is destroyed in judgment in the chaos of the returning waters.

The Greater Biblical Context of Redemption

When God safely delivered Israel from Egypt in the crossing of the Reed Sea, he overwhelmingly demonstrated his ability to redeem his people from the grip of one of the strongest nations on earth. From this time forward, the Promise Bearers would associate the covenantal name of God, *Yahweh*, with *redemption*.

Indeed, God would continue to be known as a Redeemer God. Centuries later, God redeemed his people again—this time from their exile in Babylon. The prophet Isaiah talked about this later redemption as being like a new Exodus: God rescuing his people and bringing them through the desert to the Promised Land once again—

> *Comfort, comfort my people, says your God.*
> *2 Speak tenderly to Jerusalem,*
> *and cry to her*
> *that her warfare is ended,*
> *that her iniquity is pardoned,*
> *that she has received from the Lord's hand*
> *double for all her sins.*
> *3 A voice cries:*
> *"In the wilderness prepare the way of the Lord;*
> *make straight in the desert a highway for our God.*
> *4 Every valley shall be lifted up,*
> *and every mountain and hill be made low;*

> *the uneven ground shall become level,*
> *and the rough places a plain." (Isaiah 40:1-4)*

In the New Testament, Mark 1:3 quotes from Isaiah's prophecy of the new Exodus and relates it to the coming of Jesus —

> *"Behold, I send my messenger before your face,*
> *who will prepare your way,*
> *3 the voice of one crying in the wilderness:*
> *'Prepare the way of the Lord, make his paths straight,'"*
> *(Mark 1:3, quoting from Isaiah 40:3)*

By doing this, Mark is saying that the broader redemptive context of the Exodus includes Jesus. Just as God once redeemed his people from slavery in Egypt and from exile in Babylon, so God has also delivered his people from sin in Christ. In this way, the sacrifices of the Passover lamb in the first Exodus, and the atoning sacrifice of the Suffering Servant in the second Exodus, find their fulfillment in Christ's atonement on the Cross.

The Covenant is Renewed

Immediately after God delivered the Israelites from Egypt, he led them to Mount Sinai to renew the covenant God first made with their father, Abraham (Exodus 19). Previously, God had walked with Israel as a family; now, God would walk with Israel as a nation.

This is why the renewed covenant took the form of a kingship treaty. Specifically, as some scholars have noticed, it follows the format of a kingship treaty known as a *'suzerain treaty.'* A suzerain is the title for a great and all-powerful king to whom a vassal people pledged themselves and agreed to live under his stipulations. By taking the format of a suzerain treaty, the Law was emphasizing the sovereignty and power of God as a suzerain 'Great King' over Israel.

The Gift of the Law

As Israel's king, God gave his people a Law to live by. The prologue to this Law is the Ten Commandments, a summary of the entire Law (Exodus 20:1-17, Deuteronomy 5:6-21). Israel was a new nation composed of former slaves. These 'ten words' gave the Israelites the basic principles they needed to form a stable society—emphasizing such things as regular worship (20:2-11), respect for parents, reverence for life, the sacredness of marriage, the right of property ownership and the safeguarding of a judicial system by not committing perjury (20:12-16).

The rest of the Law builds upon the Ten Commandments by giving specific examples of righteous behavior. The Israelites were to return lost oxen, conduct fair trials, cancel debts every seven years and provide cities of refuge for those who committed accidental manslaughter—among many other things.

They were also to gather together regularly for the weekly Sabbath (Exodus 20:8-11, 23:12) and for such annual events as the Passover (Exodus 12:14, Numbers 9:1-5) and the Feasts of Unleavened Bread, Weeks, Tabernacles (Exodus 23:14-17) and the Day of Atonement (Leviticus 16).

Most importantly, the Law also detailed the offerings that were to be made in worship. There were several types of offerings, not just one. First, came the offerings for sins—the sin offering (Leviticus 4:1-5:13) and the guilt offering (Leviticus 5:14-6:7). Secondly, were those offerings used to express personal consecration and devotion—the burnt offering (Leviticus 1) and the grain offering (Leviticus 2). Thirdly, was the peace offering, used either to express thanksgiving, to fulfill a vow or as a freewill act of worship (Leviticus 3).

Hebrews 10:1-18 argues that "it is impossible for the blood of bulls and goats to take away sins" (verse 4) and that God has "neither desired nor taken pleasure in sacrifices and offerings and burnt offerings and sin offerings" (verse 8). It then speaks of Christ who has come "to do your will" (verse 9) and who offered "for all time a single sacrifice for sins" (verse 12). In this way, the various animal offerings made in the Old Testament era found their completion in Christ.

The Golden Calf

Despite God's gift of the Law, the Israelites swiftly fell into idolatry by making and worshipping an idolatrous golden calf (Exodus 32). Appalled at this sudden lapse of obedience to God as their king, Moses pleaded with God not to destroy the nation in judgment.

This story of the golden calf is very important for understanding the biblical metanarrative. God used the occasion to provide the fullest self-description of his character so far in the Bible. The Chosen People would learn that God is not only gracious but also holy and must be respected as such—

> [5] *The LORD descended in the cloud and stood with him there, and proclaimed the name of the LORD.* [6] *The LORD passed before him and proclaimed, "The LORD, the LORD, a God merciful and gracious, slow to anger, and abounding in steadfast love and faithfulness,* [7] *keeping steadfast love for thousands, forgiving iniquity and transgression and sin, but who will by no means clear the guilty, visiting the iniquity of the fathers on the children and the children's children, to the third and the fourth generation." (Exodus 34:5-7)*

Being gracious, God is faithful, forgiving and merciful (verses 6-7), yet, being holy, God is also judging (verse 7). This tension between grace and holiness reverberates through the rest of the Bible, as God will repeatedly judge yet also redeem Israel. The tension achieves its ultimate resolution in the Bible in the atonement of Christ, when the demands of God's lawful holiness become satisfied in the atoning mercy of God's love, thereby reconciling us to God (Romans 5:8-11).

The Tent of Meeting

The Law also instructed the Israelites to construct a tent of meeting as their place of worship (Exodus 25-30:11; chapters 36-40).

The tent of meeting depicts God's plan of redemption. Humanity had been expelled from Eden, away from God's Presence (Genesis 3:23-24). But the priests' garments worn in the tent of meeting were decorated with pomegranates, symbolic of God's holy garden (Exodus 28:33); also, the Presence of God dwelled there, as in Eden (Exodus 25:8). The tent of meeting was a physical reminder of God's ultimate plan to restore humanity to Eden.

The tent of meeting also speaks of the Incarnation. God's Presence in the tent is described as a cloud filled with glory—

> *"Then the cloud covered the tent of meeting, and the glory of the LORD filled the tabernacle" (Exodus 40:34).*

The Hebrews called this glory cloud, the *Shekinah* cloud, from a Hebrew word meaning, 'to dwell.' Later, John would liken Jesus as being a tent of meeting filled with the Shekinah glory cloud. This becomes apparent in a more literal translation of the original Greek of John 1:14—

> *And the Word became flesh, and did tabernacle among us, and we beheld his glory, glory as of an only begotten of a father, full of grace and truth. (John 1:14, Young's Literal Translation).*

Summary of Chapter Four

The book of Exodus began with Israel in bondage, seemingly abandoned by God. It ends with a merciful and holy God dwelling in their midst as they journey together into the wilderness (Exodus 40:34-38). During the next forty years, Israel will learn about obeying and trusting in God, her Redeemer.

5 Israel in the Wilderness

We may ask, "Why was it was necessary, in God's redemptive plan, for the Promise Bearers to become a nation?" One answer is so that God could become known to the world as a king. Israel was meant to, "Declare his glory among the nations, his marvelous works among all the peoples" (1 Chronicles 16:24). Israel was to display the reign of God by being a "kingdom of priests" and a "holy nation"—a different people having no king but God (Exodus 19:6).

The surrounding nations would marvel at this unique, holy nation having no king except for the Lord God. The nations would see God in action, working on behalf of his people by protecting and providing for them and blessing them. God would be glorified among the nations as he governed and defended his people, his "treasured possession" (Exodus 19:5). This is why the Psalmist sings hopefully: "Nations will fear the name of the LORD, and all the kings of the earth will fear your glory" (Psalm 102:15).

To experience the living God like this, all that Israel had to do was to remain faithful to the covenant. They were to be *tāmiim* in keeping this Law—a Hebrew word meaning 'blameless' or 'completely faithful' (Genesis 17:1, Psalm 15:2). If they were *tāmiim* in their love for God, he would guide them, bless them and provide for them as their king.

It was in the Sinai wilderness, over a period of forty years, that Israel, the nation of the Promise Bearers, was taught to trust and obey God and to be faithful to him as her king. The stories of

Israel's wilderness journeys and the teachings given to her are found in *Exodus*, *Leviticus*, *Numbers* and *Deuteronomy*.

A number of important themes stand out from these books for understanding the plan of God in the Bible as a whole. In this chapter we'll look briefly at what God taught Israel about holiness, the providence of God, the coming of kingship and the coming ministry of the prophets.

Holiness

A main purpose of the book of *Leviticus* was to instruct Israel to be a holy nation. Since God is a holy God, the Israelites must be a holy people as well. In teaching about holiness, however, Leviticus has a tension within it between the total holiness of God and the imperfection of the people of God.

Israel was to be holy by making offerings to God (Leviticus 1-7 and 16-17). At the heart of Israel's pursuit of holiness would be atonement through sacrifice. God is the only source of holiness.

Israel was also to be holy by separating herself from an impure world. Much of Leviticus is an expanded application of the Ten Commandments, which set Israel apart *ethically* from her neighbors. Furthermore, the food laws, which distinguished 'clean' from 'unclean' foods, also set Israel apart *ethnically* from other nations by forbidding some foods common to others (Leviticus 11). But, as much as Israel separated herself from an impure world, impurity would still prove to remain in her heart.

In Leviticus, holiness was also symbolized by physical perfection. The animals for sacrifice had to be without blemish while the priests making those sacrifices had to be without deformity (Leviticus 21:16-23). Similarly, a woman who gave birth had to be ritually purified from the blood of the birth (Leviticus 12). Leviticus is not denigrating people with deformities or postpartum women. These laws regarding ceremonial imperfection seem to have been done out of the people's sense of honoring God by presenting their physical best. Blood, seen as representing life, was especially treated with care.

In the time of Jesus, the Pharisees continued to adhere to the holiness laws of Leviticus, especially by separating themselves from those whom they considered to be impure. Jesus, on the other hand, did not separate himself from impure people. Rather, he drew near to them and made them physically and spiritually whole. He practiced holiness in a different way from the Pharisees because his atoning sacrifice makes us holy, even as it says:

> *For our sake he made him to be sin who knew no sin, so that in him we might become the righteousness of God (2 Corinthians 5:21).*

Because Jesus' atoning death makes us holy, we no longer have to separate ourselves from imperfect people as we seek God. Instead, we can work for their redemption just as Jesus did. In this way, Jesus resolves the tension between the total holiness of God and the utter imperfection of humanity found in Leviticus' laws of holiness—thus fulfilling them.

Providence

Another important theme from Israel's years in the wilderness is the providence of God.

The book of *Numbers* is so-named because it begins with the numbering of the warriors of Israel. But perhaps a more appropriate title would be *The Book of Complaints* since it is full of the Israelites' repeated grumblings against God's providential care. Although they had experienced the Exodus, their constant complaining about their situation fueled a spirit of distrust toward God for their future. Their faithlessness became so intolerable that they even disobeyed God's command to take possession of the Promised Land (Numbers 14). God passed judgment on them by consigning that generation—the one which had experienced the Exodus—to remain in the wilderness until it all died out.

Israel's failure in the wilderness contrasts with Jesus' trust in God's providence in the Judean desert (Matthew 4:1-11, Mark 1:12-13, Luke 4:1-13). While Israel complained and rebelled against God, Jesus entrusted himself fully to the care of his Heavenly Father. In his replies to Satan, Jesus quotes directly from Israel's wilderness story—emphasizing that where Israel failed, Jesus triumphed (Deuteronomy 8:3, 6:16. 6:13). He is the 'new Israel' who is able to do what old Israel could not.

The Coming of the Kings

In the wilderness, God ruled directly over his people in a true theocracy, but the account also speaks of a day when God would rule indirectly over them through kings: theocracy being modified to include human kingship. This was part of God's plan from the very beginning, a plan that eventually culminated in the coming of the Messiah-King.

Even as early as Abraham we find hints of the coming of kingship when Abraham is told, "kings shall come from you" (Genesis 17:6; see also 17:16, 35:11). Jacob also prophesied early on that the tribe of Judah would be the seat of this kingship—

> *The scepter shall not depart from Judah, nor the ruler's staff from between his feet, until tribute comes to him; and to him shall be the obedience of the peoples. (Genesis 49:10)*

When we read the account of Israel in the wilderness, it also reaffirms this promise of kingship—

> *"When you come to the land that the LORD your God is giving you, and you possess it and dwell in it and then say, 'I will set a king over me, like all the nations that are around me,' 15 you may indeed set a king over you whom the LORD your God will choose. One from among*

your brothers you shall set as king over you. You may not put a
foreigner over you, who is not your brother. (Deuteronomy 17:14-15)

Kingship for Israel is also mentioned in Balaam's prophecy. Balaam was a pagan seer who was hired by the king of Moab to curse Israel as she travelled in the wilderness (Numbers 22-24). Balaam found himself unable to curse a nation he knew God had blessed, so he blessed them instead in a series of prophecies which culminate in a prediction of a coming ruler in Israel:

> *I see him, but not now;*
> *I behold him, but not near:*
> *a star shall come out of Jacob,*
> *and a scepter shall rise out of Israel;*
> *it shall crush the forehead of Moab*
> *and break down all the sons of Sheth.*
> *18 Edom shall be dispossessed;*
> *Seir also, his enemies, shall be dispossessed.*
> *Israel is doing valiantly.*
> *19 And one from Jacob shall exercise dominion*
> *and destroy the survivors of cities! (Number 24:17-19)*

Many understand this to be a prediction of King David, who as a warrior defeated Moab and Edom (2 Samuel 8). But since David's victories were temporary, the prophecy seems also to find a greater fulfillment in the coming promised Redeemer.

Psalms 2 and 110 describe this anointed Messiah-King as one who will permanently rule the nations—using such words as:

> *Why do the nations rage*
> *and the peoples plot in vain?*
> *2 The kings of the earth set themselves,*
> *and the rulers take counsel together,*
> *against the LORD and against his Anointed, saying,*
> *3 "Let us burst their bonds apart*
> *and cast away their cords from us." (Psalm 2:1-3)*

> *The LORD says to my Lord:*

> *"Sit at my right hand,*
> *until I make your enemies your footstool." (Psalm 110:1)*

All of this indicates that kingship was part of God's plan for his people all along. When the kings of Israel finally did come, they were expected to rule as God's anointed viceroys: living under the Law of God, not above it, and ruling humbly, not arrogantly like the other kings of the world (Deuteronomy 17:18-20). This ideal to which the kings of Israel were called was fulfilled ultimately in the Messiah.

The Coming of the Prophets

Besides speaking of the coming of the kings, the wilderness accounts also tell of the coming of the prophets, who would speak God's words and to whom the people were to pay heed. Moses mentions their coming in Deuteronomy 18:15-22. In verse 15 he says—

> *The LORD your God will raise up for you a prophet like me from among you, from your brothers—it is to him you shall listen.*

Verse 20 makes it clear that the *office* of prophet is being spoken of, rather than a single prophet, with each prophet being tested—

> (God is speaking) *"But the prophet who presumes to speak a word in my name that I have not commanded him to speak, or who speaks in the name of other gods, that same prophet shall die."*

We commonly think of a prophet as someone who predicts the future. In reality, the biblical prophets were advocates for the covenant. God's covenant with Israel was like a business contract. God sent the prophets to remind his people of the terms of the contract.

Those contract terms are found in Deuteronomy 28-30. The terms stipulate the blessings that would come for keeping the covenant and the curses that would follow for disobedience. Explicit warnings are given for persistent defiance: their harvests would fail, they would be defeated in battle and, eventually, they would be cast into exile (Deuteronomy 28:15-68).

The preaching of the prophets is based on these contract terms of the covenant. The stringent preaching of the prophets may come across to us as being judgmental and dour; in reality the prophets were simply doing their job as covenant spokespersons by warning the people of the consequences of their behavior (2 Kings 17:13). For this reason the terms of the covenant found in Deuteronomy 28-30 are especially important for understanding the prophetical books of the Bible.

One other thing about the prophets needs to be stressed: when Moses spoke of the coming of the prophets in Deuteronomy 18, implicit in his words, though not openly stated, is the reality that the prophets would suffer whenever the people rejected their prophecies. In the least, the prophets would be scorned. At the worse, they would be killed. They would be suffering servants. As 2 Chronicles 36:15-16 puts it —

> The LORD, the God of their fathers, sent persistently to them by his messengers, because he had compassion on his people and on his dwelling place. 16 But they kept mocking the messengers of God, despising his words and scoffing at his prophets, until the wrath of the LORD rose against his people, until there was no remedy.

This ties into the theme of the Suffering Servant in the Bible. We first encounter this theme in the prophecy of the 'First Gospel' of Genesis 3:15, when the serpent is told it will strike the heel of the Promised Redeemer. We next saw the theme epitomized in the sufferings of Joseph. Now we see it in the prophets. And we will see it again in the Suffering Servant of Isaiah 53 — words that Jesus would apply directly to himself.

Summary of Chapter Five

Over a period of forty years in the wilderness, God shaped Israel to be a nation for himself by teaching them that they were to be devoted to him as their king. Despite all this effort, in God's eyes they continued to be a "stubborn people" (Deuteronomy 9:6). Yet, compared to how corrupt Israel would later become, her time in the wilderness would seem like halcyon days. Looking back, God said sadly through the prophet Jeremiah:

> *"I remember the devotion of your youth*
> *your love as a bride,*
> *how you followed me in the wilderness,*
> *in a land not sown.*
> *3 Israel was holy to the LORD,*
> *the firstfruits of his harvest."*
> *(Jeremiah 2:2-3a)*

God had revealed himself as a king to his people, Israel, and had done all that could be done to prepare Israel to be a nation. Now, it was up to her to fulfill her purpose of displaying the kingdom of God to the world.

6 *Israel as a Nation*

The ultimate purpose of Israel as a nation was to demonstrate the kingdom of God to the world. She was meant to call the nations to the Lord God by transcending her own ethno-centricity, displaying the glory and power of God in her midst and drawing the surrounding peoples to God. This would be in fulfillment of God's promise to Abraham that "in you all the families of the earth shall be blessed"— a promise that we find reiterated time and again (Genesis 12:3, 18:18, 22:18, 26:4, 28:14).

The prophet Isaiah also bore witness to this national purpose for Israel in such words as:

> *It shall come to pass in the latter days*
> *that the mountain of the house of the LORD*
> *shall be established as the highest of the mountains,*
> *and shall be lifted up above the hills;*
> *and all the nations shall flow to it,*
> *3 and many peoples shall come, and say:*
> *"Come, let us go up to the mountain of the LORD,*
> *to the house of the God of Jacob,*
> *that he may teach us his ways*
> *and that we may walk in his paths."*
> *For out of Zion shall go the law,*
> *and the word of the LORD from Jerusalem. (Isaiah 2:2-3)*

At times, Israel partially succeeded in fulfilling this calling. We catch glimpses of it during the reigns of kings like David, Solomon, Hezekiah and Josiah—such as when the queen of Sheba came to see the glory of Solomon's reign and she blessed the Lord (1 Kings 10). And we see suggestions of it in the ministries of prophets like Elijah and Elisha—such as when

Naaman, the commander of the Syrian army, came to be cured of leprosy and was drawn to the God of Israel (2 Kings 5).

For the most part, however, Israel failed in her task. She seemed more preoccupied with her own ethnic self-preservation than with proclaiming God's glory among the nations. A perfect example is seen in Jonah's heartless reluctance to preach to Nineveh, Israel's arch-enemy.

The Bible repeatedly mentions Israel failure to fulfill her purpose. From the years of her desert wanderings to the days of the judges and kings, all the way up to her return from exile, Israel is depicted as repeatedly failing in her calling. This void created a longing and anticipation in the Old Testament for the Messiah to come.

Of the many themes we are found in the stories of Israel as a nation, four are especially important for understanding the biblical metanarrative. They are: (1) the Land, (2) the Leadership, (3) the Wisdom Tradition and (4) the Temple.

THE LAND

To be a nation, the Israelites needed their own land. The days of wandering in the wilderness were only meant to be temporary. God decreed that the land of Canaan would be their inheritance.

The Bible often uses that word 'inheritance' (Hebrew: *nachalah*) when it speaks of Israel's land. It does this to emphasize that the land came to Israel as a gift from God. We should keep in mind, however, that the Bible also uses the same word to describe God's distribution of land to *all* the nations, not just Israel, to indicate that God owns all the earth—

The Most High gave to the nations their inheritance
when he divided mankind,
he fixed the borders of the peoples … (Deuteronomy 32:8)

As for Israel, four hundred years before she inherited the land of Canaan, God had told Abraham that it would happen:

> 13 Then the LORD said to Abram, "Know for certain that your offspring will be sojourners in a land that is not theirs and will be servants there, and they will be afflicted for four hundred years. … 16 And they shall come back here in the fourth generation, for the iniquity of the Amorites is not yet complete." (Genesis 15:13, 16)

Four hundred years later, the time had come. As Israel was about to enter Canaan, Moses recalled the previous word which had been given to Abraham—

> Not because of your righteousness or the uprightness of your heart are you going in to possess their land, but because of the wickedness of these nations the LORD your God is driving them out from before you, and that he may confirm the word that the LORD swore to your fathers, to Abraham, to Isaac, and to Jacob. (Deuteronomy 9:5)

Many people who read the Bible today are troubled by Israel's conquest of Canaan. They see it as an ethnic cleansing that is incompatible with a God of mercy and redemption.

Indeed, it is difficult to understand the conquest until we recall the wider context of who God is and what God is doing. As the Creator, God alone owns the nations and the lands they occupy. As the Judge of the world, God has the right to remove an unjust people from the land. We often overlook these fundamental assertions.

Canaan had become utterly detestable to the Lord God (Leviticus 20:22-23, Deuteronomy 8; 18:9-14). Any co-existence of Israel with Canaan would have surely corrupted the fragile knowledge of God which the Israelites had gained. God's ultimate mission to redeem the world was more important than the continuation of Canaan as a corrupt, idolatrous nation. So, Canaan fell under judgment. It was God's war, not Israel's, with almost all the people of Canaan hardening their hearts and refusing to turn to the Lord God (Joshua 11:20).

When we keep the broader redemptive purposes of God in mind, however, we must also realize that Israel's inheritance must refer to something more than just an ethnic homeland—or else God would be no more than a tribal deity. God's promise to Abraham was that, "in you all the families of the earth shall be blessed" (Genesis 12:3). Because of this promise, the final inheritance of the redeemed people of God must, in some way, be greater than a piece of land belonging only to one people.

Indeed, in the New Testament, the land of Israel symbolizes our eternal redemption. Hebrew 4:1-11 sees Israel's land as representing the ceaseless Seventh Day in the Garden of Eden. Returning to God's Garden is the ultimate inheritance of the people of God.

The New Testament teaches that this final inheritance is acquired in Christ. "In him we have obtained an inheritance," Paul writes (Ephesians 1:11). Similarly, 1 Peter 1:3-4 says:

> *According to his great mercy, he has caused us to be born again to a living hope through the resurrection of Jesus Christ from the dead, 4 to an inheritance that is imperishable, undefiled, and unfading, kept in heaven for you.*

The gift of the Holy Spirit to the believer is, "the guarantee of our inheritance until we acquire possession of it" (Ephesians 1:14).

But this return to paradise will only be possible to those who love God; all who love evil will be excluded, just as the Canaanites were. In the last chapter of the Bible we catch of glimpse of those who are allowed entrance and those who are not:

> *Blessed are those who wash their robes, so that they may have the right to the tree of life and that they may enter the city by the gates. 15 Outside are the dogs and sorcerers and the sexually immoral and*

murderers and idolaters, and everyone who loves and practices falsehood. (Revelation 22:14-15)

THE LEADERSHIP: Joshua and the Judges

Much of the history of Israel as a nation is recorded in *Joshua, Judges, 1 and 2 Samuel* and *1 and 2 Kings*. In the Hebrew Bible these books are called the *'Former Prophets.'* Our English Bibles lack this designation. We just consider these books to be historical, but not prophetic. But once we realize that a prophet was a spokesperson for God's covenant, we can see why these histories are considered to be prophetic. Like the prophets, they warned and encouraged Israel to keep the covenant.

So, for example, *Joshua* recounts Israel's initial campaign against Canaan under the leadership of Joshua. It emphasizes that Joshua was successful in his campaigns because he was faithful to the covenant (Joshua 1:7, 23:5-13, 24:31).

Judges, the second book in the Former Prophets, records the leadership of the 'judges' (Hebrew: *'shāphatim'*). They were anointed rulers whom God raised up to administer justice by delivering Israel from oppression and by deciding judicial cases. As administers of justice they were forerunners of the kings who would come later.

The book of Judges emphasizes how Israel failed to complete the conquest of Canaan because of her repeated faithlessness to God. The book narrates twelve cycles of decay and deliverance in which Israel: (1) abandons God, (2) falls under oppression, (3) cries out for deliverance and (4) is delivered by a judge sent from God. Yet, despite Israel's recurring infidelity, God remained faithful to the covenant.

The last five chapters of Judges describe in hideous detail the moral depravity into which Israel had fallen without a king (Joshua 17-21). The purpose in doing this is to cause the reader to value King David and his successors. The final words are a note of thankfulness that a king of David was now on the throne:

> *In those days there was no king in Israel. Everyone did what was right in his own eyes. (Judges 21:25, see also 17:6, 18:1, 19:1)*

This also explains the inclusion of the story of Abimelech, the godless son of Gideon (Judges 9). Again, the author of Judges is deliberately contrasting this disastrous pseudo-king with the later divinely-appointed kings of David.

Since the book of Judges causes us to value the house of David, then it also indirectly makes us value the Messiah, whose reign, as we shall see, would be greater and more perfect than David's.

THE LEADERSHIP: The 'Kingship Problem'

1 Samuel is the third book of the Former Prophets. It describes how Israel came to be led by kings.

Samuel was a man between the times—he lived in the era of the judges yet he anointed the first two kings of Israel: Saul and David. Samuel also set the tone for what a godly king should be.

In the time of the judges, Israel was a strict theocracy with no king other than God, who ruled through the words of the Law and through the prophets and judges whom he raised up. Still, the people wanted to have their own king "like all the nations" (1 Samuel 8:20).

This led to the 'kingship problem.' Although the people rejected God as their king (1 Samuel 8:7-8), God still was such. How would God rule over Israel?

The solution to this kingship problem was for God to appoint a viceroy—a godly king who would rule in God's stead and do God's will. Such a person would not be like the kings of the nations. Instead of being a law unto himself like those kings, he would be subservient to the Law of God (Deuteronomy 17:18-

20). And instead of being an arrogant king of the world, he was expected to be humble and listen to God's prophets (2 Samuel 12). As a representative of God, the king was supposed to rule with righteousness and justice and wisdom. This was the paradigm to which the kings of Israel were called, but just as Israel often failed to live up to her ideal, so would all her kings, to a lesser or greater degree.

The first king whom God raised up for Israel was Saul—a man who fell far short of the mark. His appointment was not a mistake on God's part, but it seems to have been a deliberate choice meant to show the difference between a worldly king, which is what the people wanted, and a godly viceroy (1 Samuel 12:14-17).

THE LEADERSHIP: David, the Godly King

The second king chosen by God was David. Unlike Saul, David knew the Lord and was said to be a man after God's own heart (1 Samuel 13:14).

The David Stories occupy a considerable amount of the Bible (1 Samuel 16-31, 2 Samuel, 1 Kings 1-2, 1 Chronicles 11-29). In addition, we also find many of David's psalms and even a story about his great-grandparents (Ruth). But the most important of all this material about David concerns God's promise to establish his house as an everlasting dynasty—

> The LORD declares to you that the LORD will make you a house. …
> 16 And your house and your kingdom shall be made sure forever before me. Your throne shall be established forever.'" (2 Samuel 7:11b, 16)

Not only did God promise David that his dynasty would endure forever, but God also expected every king in David's dynasty to follow the ideal of being a godly viceroy. If a king from the house of David did not fear God, he would be disciplined:

12 When your days are fulfilled and you lie down with your fathers, I will raise up your offspring after you, who shall come from your body, and I will establish his kingdom. 13 He shall build a house for my name, and I will establish the throne of his kingdom forever. 14 I will be to him a father, and he shall be to me a son. When he commits iniquity, I will discipline him with the rod of men, with the stripes of the sons of men, 15 but my steadfast love will not depart from him, as I took it from Saul, whom I put away from before you. (2 Samuel 7:12-15)

This promise made to David, and the expectation that each king from the house of David would be a godly viceroy, is extremely significant for understanding the biblical metanarrative. From this, the hope that God would send the Messiah really began to develop. It is of little surprise, then, that the Old Testament often looks back to God's promise given to David as foundational (2 Samuel 22:51; 1 Kings 2:4, 45; 1 Chronicles 22:10, 28:6-7; 2 Chronicles 6:16, 7:18, 13:5, 21:7, Psalm 89:3-4, 29-37; Isaiah 9:2-7; Jeremiah 33:14-21; Daniel 7:27).

The New Testament also looks back to God's promise to David. One example would be the words of the angel Gabriel to Mary—

"And behold, you will conceive in your womb and bear a son, and you shall call his name Jesus. 32 He will be great and will be called the Son of the Most High. And the Lord God will give to him the throne of his father David, 33 and he will reign over the house of Jacob forever, and of his kingdom there will be no end." (Luke 1:31-33)

Another example would be in Paul's preaching—

… (God) raised up David to be their king, of whom he testified and said, 'I have found in David the son of Jesse a man after my heart, who will do all my will.' 23 Of this man's offspring God has brought to Israel a Savior, Jesus, as he promised. (Acts 13:22-23)

Up to this point, the biblical metanarrative has been shaped by three major promises:

(1) The Promise of the 'First Gospel' (Genesis 3:15)

(2) The Promise to Abraham (Genesis 12:1-3)

(3) The Promise to David (2 Samuel 7:4-17)

The first promise is that God would send a Redeemer. The second promise is that a redemptive blessing would come to the world through Abraham's family, the chosen people. The third promise is that David's dynasty would be everlasting. From these expectations grew the hope of a Messiah.

Israel itself was not the Messiah, as some mistakenly say. This is because the house of David, from which the Messiah-Redeemer would come, is just a family within Israel. Keep in mind that the Bible is not primarily a history of Israel. Rather, it depicts God's self-revelation to the world through a chosen people that culminates in the coming of a Redeemer.

THE LEADERSHIP: When the Kings Ruled

1 Samuel, as we have seen, describes how kingship came to Israel. The fourth book in the Former Prophets is *2 Samuel*, which is a history of David. It portrays him as a godly, though deeply flawed, king.

Besides telling of his achievements and his trust in God, 2 Samuel also speaks of David's sin. The matter of Bathsheba and Uriah is not glossed over but openly reported (2 Samuel 11-12), while the consequences flowing from David's foolish choices are brutally emphasized (2 Samuel 13-24). 2 Samuel does this to show that, despite the promise given to David that he would have an everlasting dynasty, he was as much in need of God's atoning mercy as anyone else.

1 and 2 Kings, the final books in the Former Prophets, tell the stories of all the kings who came after David. Since 1 and 2 Kings are prophetic in nature—in the sense of warning the nation to keep their covenant with God—they associate the decline of the nation to its persistent unfaithfulness to the covenant.

The narration begins with Solomon, whose reign was a moment of glory for Israel, a seeming fulfillment of her purpose to display the glory of God to the world (1 Kings 1-10). But sin marred Solomon's reign (1 Kings 11) and the rebellion of the northern tribes after Solomon's death shattered Israel's ability to attract the nations to God (1 Kings 12).

The ensuing chapters record the reigns of all the kings of the fractured nation, those of Israel in the north and Judah in the south. When a king emulated the ideal of being a godly viceroy, the account says that he "did what was right in the eyes of the LORD." And when he fell far short of the mark, the summary account of his life was that "he did what was evil in the sight of the LORD."

While the main focus of 1 and 2 Kings is on the various kings, the books also mention the ministries of some of the prophets. Those sent to the northern kingdom of Israel included Elijah (1 Kings 17-19, 21; 2 Kings 1-2), and Elisha (1 Kings 19; 2 Kings 2-9; 13), Ahijah (1 Kings 14), Micaiah (1 Kings 22) and Jonah (2 Kings 14:25). Others of the northern prophets, such as Amos and Hosea, are not mentioned at all.

Similarly, Isaiah, who was sent to the southern kingdom of Judah, is mentioned (2 Kings 19-20) but there is no mention made of the other southern prophets: Joel, Jeremiah, Ezekiel, Habakkuk or Zephaniah. Clearly, there was heavy prophetic activity, only some of which was recorded by the author of 1 and 2 Kings.

Despite the labors of the prophets, the divided nation continued to decline until the northern tribes of Israel were exiled in 722 BC (2 Kings 17), followed by Judah in 586 BC (2 Kings 25). The Law clearly warned about the possibility of exile as an ultimate punishment, in Leviticus 26:33 and Deuteronomy 28:63-64.

THE LEADERSHIP: Longing Grows for the Messiah

God intended Israel to be a kingdom of priests ruled by a godly viceroy. Together, they would display the power and splendor of God to the world. The failure of Israel and her kings to fulfill this expectation explains why the longing grew for a Messiah who would finally usher in the kingdom of God (Psalm 2; 110; Isaiah 7– 9:7, 11:1-9; Isaiah 53; Micah 5:2; see also Jeremiah 31:31-34).

This king would be a *māshiach* (Hebrew), an *'anointed one.'* All the kings from the house of David were considered to be 'anointed ones,' but the coming Anointed One would be a *Māshiach* above all the other kings of Judah.

Psalm 2 especially exemplifies the budding anticipation for this *Māshiach*, the *Messiah*. It reads, in part—

> 2 *The kings of the earth set themselves,*
> *and the rulers take counsel together,*
> *against the LORD and against his Anointed, saying,*
> 3 *"Let us burst their bonds apart*
> *and cast away their cords from us." ...*
> 7 *I will tell of the decree:*
> *The LORD said to me, "You are my Son;*
> *today I have begotten you.*
> 8 Ask of me, and I will make the nations your heritage,*
> *and the ends of the earth your possession." (Psalm 2:2-3, 7-8)*

The New Testament freely uses Psalm 2 to identify Jesus as the Messiah, as we shall see in chapter eight.

THE WISDOM TRADITION

Aside from the land and the leadership, a third major theme regarding Israel as a nation was her wisdom tradition. In the ancient Near East, when a nation was stabile enough to allow for reflection and learning, it would often produce 'wisdom writings.' Frequently, these writings were associated with kings or others in leadership. For instance, we read of Daniel and his companions who were taught "the literature and language of the Chaldeans" before entering royal service in Babylon (Daniel 1:4, 20). Other examples can be found from Egypt, such as in the Egyptian wisdom writing known as the *Instruction of King Amenemhet I*.

Israel also had her wisdom writings, which added to her national identity. These are seen in the reflective texts of the Old Testament known as *Job, Proverbs, Ecclesiastes, Song of Solomon* and a few psalms, such as *Psalm 1*.

However, the wisdom tradition in Israel was different in kind from that of her neighbors. In Babylon and Egypt, wisdom was based on education and the insight of their sages. In Israel, wisdom among her sages began with submission to God, just as seen in the Garden of Eden concerning the knowledge of good and evil (Genesis 3). Proverbs reflects this in the famous saying—

> *The fear of the LORD is the beginning of wisdom, and the knowledge of the Holy One is insight (Proverbs 9:10).*

Biblical theologians have wondered how the wisdom writings of the Old Testament fit into God's redemptive plan. Other books of Scripture tell how God promised that a Redeemer would come from a chosen people. But the wisdom writings do not readily seem to fit into this progression. They're not about what God is doing so much as what the people of Israel should do in their everyday lives under the covenant. They speak of such practical matters as dealing with troublesome people, making sense of suffering and kindling a romance. They're not laws taught by priests, or oracles spoken by prophets, but the practical teachings of sages meant to help the faithful in Israel in the art of living.

So, how do such writings fit in with God's plan of salvation for the world? One suggestion is that they demonstrate that redemption is meant to engender wisdom. Salvation instills a wisdom within us that makes us whole by giving us the personal and practical insight to know how to live life well.

In the Bible, King Solomon embodies this type of wisdom, as seen in the stories about him (1 Kings 3-4) and in the writings attributed to him. Solomon's wisdom faded when he abandoned God, but since he was an 'anointed one,' a *māshiach*, his imperfect wisdom previews the perfect wisdom of the coming Messiah.

Isaiah 11:1-9 portrays a coming *Māshiach* who would be wiser than Solomon. The description of his unsurpassed wisdom depicts how righteousness and justice and wholeness will flourish in the lives of all who live under his rule —

> *There shall come forth a shoot from the stump of Jesse,*
> *and a branch from his roots shall bear fruit.*
> *2 And the Spirit of the LORD shall rest upon him,*
> *the Spirit of wisdom and understanding,*
> *the Spirit of counsel and might,*
> *the Spirit of knowledge and the fear of the LORD.*
> *3 And his delight shall be in the fear of the LORD.*
> *He shall not judge by what his eyes see,*
> *or decide disputes by what his ears hear,*
> *4 but with righteousness he shall judge the poor,*
> *and decide with equity for the meek of the earth;*
> *and he shall strike the earth with the rod of his mouth,*
> *and with the breath of his lips he shall kill the wicked.*
> *5 Righteousness shall be the belt of his waist,*
> *and faithfulness the belt of his loins.*
> *6 The wolf shall dwell with the lamb,*
> *and the leopard shall lie down with the young goat,*
> *and the calf and the lion and the fattened calf together;*
> *and a little child shall lead them.*
> *7 The cow and the bear shall graze;*
> *their young shall lie down together;*
> *and the lion shall eat straw like the ox.*
> *8 The nursing child shall play over the hole of the cobra,*
> *and the weaned child shall put his hand on the adder's den.*

9 They shall not hurt or destroy
in all my holy mountain;
for the earth shall be full of the knowledge of the LORD
as the waters cover the sea.

In 1 Corinthians 1:30 Paul refers to Christ as our "wisdom from God." In saying this, Paul tapped into the wisdom tradition of the Old Testament and affirmed that Jesus the Messiah fulfills that tradition. He is the Messianic King of Isaiah 11:1-9 whose wisdom heals our lives and instills in us the godly knowledge we need to live with clarity for God in an ambiguous and broken world.

THE TEMPLE

Lastly, another major theme concerning Israel's identity as a nation is 'the temple.' In the ancient Near East, temples were essential to a nation's image. A sign that a nation was well established would be its stately, dignified temple(s).

Israel was different. For many years, her temple had been no more than a tent (2 Samuel 7:5-7). Nonetheless, upon David's request, God permitted David's son, Solomon, to build a commanding temple (2 Samuel 7:12-13). When the Temple was dedicated, the Presence of God as represented by the Shekinah glory cloud filled it, just as it had previously filled the tent of meeting (1 Kings 8:10-11, Exodus 40:35).

Every aspect of the Temple represents God. The presence of the Shekinah cloud within the physical building is a symbol of the coming Incarnation, when "the Word became flesh and dwelt among us" (John 1:14). The inclusion of a court for the Gentile nations represents God's desire that the whole world would come to know him. The Holy of Holies represents the utter holiness of God, while the sacrifices represent the need for an atonement to cleanse us from sin.

The building as a whole represents the rule of God as king over Israel, with his throne said to be in heaven and his footstool the temple in Jerusalem (1 Chronicles 28:2). Even the 400 pomegranates which adorned the Temple, which suggest the Garden of Eden, remind us of God's reign (1 Kings 7:42).

Yet, despite these different aspects by which the Temple represented God, it still was not God. The prophets reminded the people not to place their trust in a building, but to have faith in God—

Hear the word of the LORD, all you men of Judah who enter these gates to worship the LORD. 3 Thus says the LORD of hosts, the God of Israel: Amend your ways and your deeds, and I will let you dwell in this place. 4 Do not trust in these deceptive words: 'This is the temple of the LORD, the temple of the LORD, the temple of the LORD.'" (Jeremiah 7:2-4)

Thus says the LORD:
"Heaven is my throne,
and the earth is my footstool;
what is the house that you would build for me,
and what is the place of my rest?
2 All these things my hand has made,
and so all these things came to be,
declares the LORD.
But this is the one to whom I will look:
he who is humble and contrite in spirit
and trembles at my word." (Isaiah 66:1-2)

Summary of Chapter Six

Israel had her time as a nation, but she failed in her task to glorify God as her king to the nations. All of the gifts she had received from God—her land, her leadership, her wisdom tradition and her Temple—highlighted her uniqueness as a nation yet also pointed to an ideal existence greater than herself which still awaited a fulfillment.

7 *The Exile and the Restoration*

So egregious did the behavior of Israel and Judah become to God as their king that he sent his people into exile. This is the next major development in salvation history.

The Assyrians conquered the northern kingdom of Israel through a series of invasions, with the final collapse coming in 722 BC. This effectively ended the historical existence of the northern tribes, which were taken into exile. Only a few individuals who had left the northern tribes for various reasons continued on in Judah.

The Babylonians conquered Judah and led her into exile in 586 BC. With that development, the Bible shifts its focus to Judah's captivity and her eventual restoration.

As we begin this new epoch in salvation history, it is natural once more to ask the 'why' question: "In the plan of God, why did the exile have to happen?" Was it only to punish those who broke the covenant or was there a deeper purpose at work? We suggest that there was, indeed, a deeper purpose and it relates to the self-revelation of God. Through this discipline, Israel and Judah experienced God as the 'Holy One,' a phrase that the prophet Isaiah especially emphasized (29 times). But in the restoration, the Covenant People would also experience God as the 'Merciful One' and, eventually, as the 'Suffering Servant,' as we shall see.

What the Exile Meant to Judah

Judah went into exile because of her disobedience to the covenant; it was, in fact, the ultimate penalty for breaking the

Law (Leviticus 26:33, Deuteronomy 28:63-64). The exile had a devastating effect on the people of Judah: the lost of their land, so essential for nationhood; captivity in a foreign land; the destruction of the Temple ... all added to Judah's grief. The faithful would have especially mourned the lost the presence of God in the Temple. Ezekiel 10 and 11:22-25 describes how the presence of God left the Temple before its destruction.

Understand that, at that time, the Spirit of God did not normally indwell individual believers as in the New Testament era. Only a few chosen people, such as the prophets, experienced the Spirit's indwelling presence. The rest of the people experienced the presence of God chiefly in the Temple.

Psalm 84:1-2 speaks of this experience in the words—

> *How lovely is your dwelling place,*
> *O LORD of hosts!*
> *2 My soul longs, yes, faints*
> *for the courts of the LORD;*
> *my heart and flesh sing for joy*
> *to the living God. (Psalm 84:1-2)*

Similarly, the author of Psalm 42 also speaks of the same experience. He was a Temple servant who had been captured or kidnapped. From a distant land he writes mournfully of wanting to experience God in the Temple once more—

> *As a deer pants for flowing streams,*
> *so pants my soul for you, O God.*
> *2 My soul thirsts for God,*
> *for the living God.*
> *When shall I come and appear before God? (Psalm 42:1-2)*

But now this experience of God in the Temple was lost for all.

Added to all this, the exiles would also have been perplexed by doubts and questions, among them being—

'Why did this happen to us?'

'Will God forgive us?'
'Has God cast us off as his people?'
'Do we have a future as a nation?'
'What about the promises made to Abraham and David?'

With the loss of their homeland, the destruction of the Temple and departure of the presence of God within it, and the troublesome questions that beset them, Psalm 137:1 captures for us the feelings of grief which overwhelmed the remnant of Judah: "By the waters of Babylon, there we sat down and wept, when we remembered Zion."

The Rebirth of Hope

God responded to the anguish of the exiles by sending them prophets who spoke words of hope and promises of restoration. Their words were based on the covenantal stipulations of Deuteronomy 28-30. There, it not only warns of an exile, but it also speaks of the possibility of a national restoration after the exile—

"And when all these things come upon you, the blessing and the curse, which I have set before you, and you call them to mind among all the nations where the LORD your God has driven you, 2 and return to the LORD your God, you and your children, and obey his voice in all that I command you today, with all your heart and with all your soul, 3 then the LORD your God will restore your fortunes and have mercy on you, and he will gather you again from all the peoples where the LORD your God has scattered you."

(Deuteronomy 30:1-3, compare Leviticus 26:40-45)

This hope of a restoration filled the preaching of the prophets. We find it mentioned in many passages—including, but not limited to, the following:

Isaiah 10:20-12:6; chapters 40-66
Jeremiah 3:14-18, chapters 30-33
Ezekiel 36-48; Daniel 7:13-18

Hosea 2:14-23, chapters 11-14
Amos 9:11-15; Obadiah 19-21
Micah 4:1-5:5a; Zephaniah 3:9-20
Zechariah 8:1-7; chapters 9-14

The Restoration Prophecies and the Messiah

Some of the most important prophecies about the coming Messiah are embedded within these passages promising Judah's restoration. This is because the prophets saw the Messiah as completing the restoration. The passages include the following:

Major Messianic Verses Embedded in the Restoration Prophecies
The Righteous King (Isaiah 11:1-9)
The Suffering Servant (Isaiah 52:13-53:12)
The New Covenant (Jeremiah 31:31-34)
The Shepherd King (Ezekiel 34:23-24)
The Son of Man (Daniel 7:13-18)
The King from Bethlehem (Micah 5:2)
The Pierced One (Zechariah 12:10)

Other major Messianic passages which are *not* embedded in prophecies about the restoration of Judah include:

Major Messianic Passages Not Embedded in Restoration Prophecies
The 'First Gospel' (Genesis 3:15)
The Promise to Abraham (Genesis 12:2-3)
The Promise to David (2 Samuel 7:8-16)
The Messiah Psalm (Psalm 2)
The Crucifixion Psalm (Psalm 22)
The King of Zion (Psalm 110)
Immanuel (Isaiah 7:14-15, 9:1-7)

When we consider the restoration prophecies as a whole, they seem otherwise incomplete apart from Jesus. For example, the coming king of the restoration is said to be one who will rule "forever" (Micah 5:2; Ezekiel 34:23-24, 37:25). But when Judah was restored from her exile in Babylon, no king of David ruled over her, never mind one who ruled forever—until the coming of

Jesus, the son of David, he who was said to be *the king of the Jews* (Matthew 2:2, 27:11, 37; John 19:21).

The passages also mention that the remnant would return to their homeland, never to be uprooted again. But the Jews *were uprooted*: by the Romans after the Jewish rebellion of 66-70 AD and again after the Bar Kochba rebellion of 132-135 AD. However, if we understand the land as a symbol of the kingdom of God instead of an ethnic homeland, these passages were also fulfilled in Jesus, the Messiah.

The restoration passages also say that the Temple would be rebuilt (Ezekiel 40-48) and that the Shekinah cloud of glory would return to it once more (Ezekiel 43). But when the Second Temple was built, the Shekinah glory cloud never returned. Instead, the New Testament speaks of the Shekinah glory cloud indwelling Jesus the Messiah, who claimed to be the living Temple of God (John 2:19).

We previously spoke about Jesus and the Shekinah cloud from John 1:14, but let's look at that verse again more closely—

> And the Word became flesh, and did tabernacle among us, and we beheld his glory, glory as of an only begotten of a father, full of grace and truth. (John 1:14, Young's Literal Translation).

Here, the Greek word for 'did tabernacle' is *eskānōsen*. It's a cognate word that is related etymologically to the Hebrew root *sh-k-n*, the root behind *mishkan*, the Tent of Meeting, and *Shekinah*, the glory cloud in which the presence of God dwells. Through this association, John 1:14 is making a powerful theological statement: namely that Jesus is the true Sanctuary in whom dwells the *Shekinah* glory cloud.

So, we see it is impossible to make sense of the restoration prophecies apart from Jesus. He is their fulfillment. The restored nation is his Messianic kingdom. He is the promised king from the line of David. He is the restored Temple. He is the atoning sacrifice that makes us righteous. Jesus is the new Israel whose Messianic kingdom displays the kingdom of God to all nations.

Of all the restoration prophecies which speak of Jesus the Messiah, two are of particular importance: the Suffering Servant prophecy of Isaiah 53 and the Son of Man prophecy of Daniel 7. Let's look at each of them in more detail.

The Suffering Servant Prophecy

The book of Isaiah contains a number of passages about the Messiah which are known as the *'servant songs'* (42:1-7, 49:1-13, 50:4-11, 52:13-53:12). They're not actual songs—that's just the name biblical scholars have given them. They're all found within a larger prophecy that concerns Judah's restoration from exile *and also God's intended salvation of the nations* (Isaiah 40-66). This wider context is very important for correctly interpreting the servant songs.

The first servant song (42:1-7) describes the Servant as an anointed and righteous king who will lead Israel and be a light to the nations.

The second servant song (49:1-13) also depicts the Servant as being a light to the nations in the words—

> *"It is too light a thing that you should be my servant*
> *to raise up the tribes of Jacob*
> *and to bring back the preserved of Israel;*
> *I will make you as a light for the nations,*
> *that my salvation may reach to the end of the earth." (Isaiah 49:6)*

In the third servant song (50:4-11), the focus shifts to the suffering of the Servant when it mentions the shameful treatment he receives from his enemies.

The fourth servant song (52:13-53:12) depicts the Suffering Servant as he offers himself as a guilt offering to atone for sin and to heal the peoples—

Surely he took up our pain
and bore our suffering,
yet we considered him punished by God,
stricken by him, and afflicted.
5 But he was pierced for our transgressions,
he was crushed for our iniquities;
the punishment that brought us peace was on him,
and by his wounds we are healed.
6 We all, like sheep, have gone astray,
each of us has turned to our own way;
and the LORD has laid on him
the iniquity of us all. (Isaiah 53:4-6, NIV) ...

Yet it was the LORD's will to crush him and cause him to suffer,
and though the LORD makes his life an offering for sin,
he will see his offspring and prolong his days,
and the will of the LORD will prosper in his hand.
11 After he has suffered,
he will see the light of life and be satisfied;
by his knowledge my righteous servant will justify many,
and he will bear their iniquities.
12 Therefore I will give him a portion among the great,
and he will divide the spoils with the strong,
because he poured out his life unto death,
and was numbered with the transgressors.
For he bore the sin of many,
and made intercession for the transgressors.
(Isaiah 53:10-12, NIV)

Those are the four servant songs. They speak of the Suffering Servant as bringing salvation to the nations by being a light to them and by being an atoning sacrifice for them.

But when understand the four servant songs in the light of their greater context, we find an unexpected twist of significance in the songs. That context, Isaiah 40-55, identifies the bringer of salvation to the nations specifically as *God in heaven*. We see this, for example, in Isaiah 45—

"Turn to me and be saved,
all you ends of the earth;
for I am God, and there is no other.
23 By myself I have sworn,
my mouth has uttered in all integrity
a word that will not be revoked:
Before me every knee will bow;
by me every tongue will swear. *(Isaiah 45:22-23)*

For Isaiah, God in heaven is the Savior of the nations, but so is the Suffering Servant. This sharing in identities continues in the New Testament. Philippians 2:6-11 appears to be based on Isaiah's prophecy about the Suffering Servant. It identifies Jesus as the Suffering Servant yet it also uses divine language in speaking of him. We see this by comparing the last two lines of Isaiah 45:23 (underlined above and referring to God in heaven) with Philippians 2:10-11 (underlined below and referring to Jesus the Messiah)—

Who, being in very nature God, did not consider equality with
God something to be used to his own advantage;
7 rather, he made himself nothing
by taking the very nature of a servant,
being made in human likeness.
8 And being found in appearance as a man,
he humbled himself
by becoming obedient to death—
even death on a cross!

9 Therefore God exalted him to the highest place
and gave him the name that is above every name,
10 that at the name of Jesus every knee should bow,
in heaven and on earth and under the earth,
11 and every tongue acknowledge that Jesus Christ is Lord,
to the glory of God the Father. *(Philippians 2:6-11, NIV)*

Philippians 2:6-11 also links Jesus' atoning death with the atoning death of Isaiah's Suffering Servant in two ways.

First, Isaiah 53:12 speaks of the Servant as one who "poured out his soul to death" while Philippians 2:7-8 (NIV) talks about Jesus who "made himself nothing" and who "humbled himself by becoming obedient to death."

Secondly, Isaiah 53:11-12 (NIV) speaks of the resurrection and exaltation of the Servant in the words, "after he has suffered, he will see the light of life," and "I will give him a portion among the great." Similarly, Philippians 2:9 (NIV) says, "Therefore God exalted him to the highest place and gave him the name that is above every name."

So, the servant songs, when understood in their greater context, not only identify the Servant with God in heaven, but they also speak of the Servant's atoning death and resurrection. And that leads us to the following important point …

If God in heaven and the Suffering Servant share in the same identity, then mercy through atonement must be an essential part of who God is. And that means that the Incarnation, the atoning death of Jesus and his resurrection are necessary for us to know the true character of God. The self-revelation of God to the world reaches its culmination in the Servant Messiah.

The Son of Man Prophecy

In Daniel 7, the prophet Daniel has a vision of God as the "Ancient of Days" (7:9-10). Then it speaks of the coming of "one like a son of man" —

> *"I saw in the night visions,*
> *and behold, with the clouds of heaven*
> *there came one like a son of man,*
> *and he came to the Ancient of Days*
> *and was presented before him.*
> *14 And to him was given dominion*
> *and glory and a kingdom,*
> *that all peoples, nations, and languages*

> *should serve him;*
> *his dominion is an everlasting dominion,*
> *which shall not pass away,*
> *and his kingdom one*
> *that shall not be destroyed. (Daniel 7:13-14)*

Many modern scholars say that the son of man figure here is Israel because Daniel 7:18 goes in to specify that it's the 'saints' who receive the kingdom, not an individual—

> *But the saints of the Most High shall receive the kingdom and possess*
> *the kingdom forever, forever and ever.'*

But this interpretation does not explain why the prophecy mentions an individual at all. It makes better sense to think of the son of man figure as a leader who embodies his people in his person, like a king would. In this way, the passage is definitely messianic, as it has traditionally been understood to be.

Indeed, Jesus understood himself to be the 'son of man' of Daniel's vision. In Matthew 24:30 he says of his second coming—

> *They will see the Son of Man coming on the clouds of heaven with*
> *power and great glory.*

This is a direct reference to Daniel 7:13, in which the son of man comes with the clouds of heaven. Similarly, when Jesus was asked during his trial if he was the Messiah, he answered—

> *"I am, and you will see the Son of Man seated at the right hand of*
> *Power, and coming with the clouds of heaven" (Mark 14:62).*

Jesus' Great Commission in Matthew 28:18-20 is also closely related to the Son of Man prophecy of Daniel 7—

> *"All authority in heaven and on earth has been given to me. Go*
> *therefore and make disciples of all nations." (Matthew 28:18-19)*
> *And to him was given dominion*
> *and glory and a kingdom,*
> *that all peoples, nations, and languages*
> *should serve him. (Daniel 7:14)*

In the four Gospels, the title 'Son of Man' is used 78 times, always by Jesus and often in the context of his authority or his second coming. It is a Messianic title, which would make sense if Jesus understood himself to be the son of man figure of Daniel's vision. Jesus the Messiah received from God an everlasting kingdom composed of people from all nations. He is the 'new Israel' who embodies in his person all whom he has redeemed.

Through prophecies such as this about the Son of Man, and Isaiah's prophecies about the Suffering Servant, hope grew among the faithful in Judah that God would send the Messiah and that a glorious future awaited Judah when she would finally be restored as a nation.

Judah's Incomplete Restoration

After the exile, however, although a number of Jews returned to their homeland, they were frustrated at the incompleteness of their nation's restoration. They had no king of their own but remained under foreign powers. They rebuilt the Temple, but only after much delay and difficulty. When the Temple was completed, the Shekinah glory cloud did not fill it as in former times. The newly restored nation was but a shadow of its former self instead of being the glorious kingdom promised by the prophets. This caused the remnant to doubt God and to become discouraged and apathetic.

Several books of the Old Testament were written during this time of uncertainty. The exile and the partial restoration of the nation had a profound impact on the tone and content of these Scriptures.

1 and 2 Chronicles recounts the history of Israel once again, but this time with the burning questions of the post-exilic times in mind. The people were wondering ... 'Why did the exile happen?' 'Will God still send the Messiah?' 'Are we still God's covenant people?' The Chronicler sought to provide answers for these and similar questions.

He teaches clearly, for instance, that the exile happened because of the nation's disobedience. A main purpose of his history is to document how disobedience to the covenant always brought trouble, while obedience brought blessings.

The Chronicler also sought to encourage everyone by stressing that the Messiah king would surely come. He repeatedly recalls God's promise that David's dynasty would be everlasting. And he also takes care to portray David and Solomon as idealized kings—turning them into examples of what the coming Messiah would be like.

The Chronicler also emphasized that God's covenant with *all Israel* still existed. While the ten northern tribes never rejoined Judah *en masse*, many individuals from Israel did so. The Chronicler goes out of his way to record the return of these people to Judah (1 Chronicles 9:2-3, 2 Chronicles 11:13-14, 15:9, 2 Chronicles 30, 31:6, 34:9, 35:17-18).

Much more can be said about 1 and 2 Chronicles but the main point of the Chronicler is that he sought to bring encouragement and perspective to the Chosen People during a difficult and discouraging period in their history.

We see the same purpose of encouragement at work in the other Scriptures written in the post-exilic era. These would include *Daniel, Esther, Ezra, Nehemiah, Haggai, Zechariah and Malachi*.

The books of *Daniel* and *Esther* address issues facing the Jews who remained behind in Babylon and Persia, which conquered Babylon. Daniel was a leader among this Jewish community. His visions reminded his fellow Jews that God still was in charge of the nations and was working his purposes toward the coming of the Messiah. Similarly, the story of Esther taught the Jews who chose to stay in Persia that God remained their king and was able to protect them despite their vulnerability as a minority.

The books of *Haggai* and *Zechariah* were written for those exiles who had returned to Judah. The first exiles to return did so under Zerubbabel shortly after Cyrus came to power in 538 BC. Quickly, by 536 BC, these returnees laid the foundation for a new Temple (Ezra 3:8-13), but then they ceased their work when opposition arose until Darius came to power in 522 BC (Ezra 4:24). The preaching of the prophets *Haggai* and *Zechariah* broke the impasse sometime around 520 BC, causing the Second Temple to be finished in 516 BC (Ezra 6:15-16).

Some 58 years later, in 458 BC, Ezra led another large group of exiles back to Judah from Babylon, to be followed by Nehemiah and his entourage in 445 BC. The books of *Ezra* and *Nehemiah* record how the influx of these new people, along with Ezra's emphasis on teaching the Law and Nehemiah's leadership in rebuilding the walls of Jerusalem, helped the people of Judah.

Still, there was a constant struggle to maintain hope in Judah as the nation continued to be but a mere shadow of its former self and the promised Messiah had not come.

The last book in the Old Testament, *Malachi*, likely was written in Nehemiah's time, perhaps during an interlude trip he made to Persia before he came back to Jerusalem. Malachi speaks of the people of Judah doubting God's love (Malachi 1:2-5) and questioning God's ways (2:17) and saying that it was useless to serve God (3:14). In reply to these doubts, Malachi preached that the glorious kingdom which God had promised would surely come—

> *Behold, I send my messenger, and he will prepare the way before me. And the Lord whom you seek will suddenly come to his temple; and the messenger of the covenant in whom you delight, behold, he is coming, says the LORD of hosts. (Malachi 3:1)*

Here, the phrases "the Lord whom you seek" and the "messenger of the covenant" appear to be references to the Messiah. Before he comes, however, another prophet, an 'Elijah,' would appear to prepare his way—

> *Behold, I will send you Elijah the prophet before the great and awesome*
> *day of the LORD comes. (Malachi 4:1)*

With these last words of Malachi, prophecy ceased in Judah until the coming of 'Elijah'—John the Baptist—in the New Testament.

Summary of Chapter Seven

The people of Israel and Judah had gone into exile because they had failed to respect God as the Holy One. When this happened, the remnant of the nation searched their soul. Speaking to that angst, the prophets promised there would be a restoration: the people would return to their inheritance where they will build a new Temple and have a new king of David rule over them, who would be the promised Messiah.

When they were restored as a nation, the Covenant People experienced God as the 'Merciful One,' but still, the promised Messiah still did not come. It was as if the restoration was incomplete and awaiting a final fulfillment.

As we shall see, when the Messiah finally did come, his kingdom would be of a different nature than anyone had expected. Coming as the Suffering Servant, he would atone for their sins and that of the nations, ushering in a kingdom that transcends ethnicity and is "not of this world" (John 18:36). In that kingdom, there would be the final fulfillment of God's promises of redemption—one being made in the Garden (Genesis 3:15), the second given to Abraham (Genesis 12:2-3) and the third spoken to David (2 Samuel 7).

8 The Fulfillment in the Messiah

As was mentioned, the restoration of Judah after the exile proved to be incomplete and disappointing. Politically, the nation remained in a weak and shameful condition: dominated by the Persians, then by the Greeks and then by the Romans. Although the prophets spoke of a coming Messiah who would usher in the glorious kingdom of God, neither Messiah nor glorious kingdom came. Still, some persisted in the hope that one day the words of the prophets would prove true.

Waiting for the Consolation of Israel

In Luke's Gospel we read of a number of these individuals who were waiting for the Messiah to come and complete Israel's restoration—

> (Simeon) *Now there was a man in Jerusalem, whose name was Simeon, and this man was righteous and devout, waiting for the consolation of Israel, and the Holy Spirit was upon him. (Luke 2:25)*

> (Anna) *And coming up at that very hour she began to give thanks to God and to speak of him to all who were waiting for the redemption of Jerusalem. (Luke 2:38)*

> (Joseph of Arimathea) *He was looking for the kingdom of God. (Luke 23:51)*

Their expectation was based on prophecies in the Old Testament that spoke of the restoration in terms of consolation and redemption, prophecies such as—

> *Comfort, comfort my people,*
> *says your God.*

2 Speak tenderly to Jerusalem,
and proclaim to her
that her hard service has been completed,
that her sin has been paid for,
that she has received from the LORD's hand
double for all her sins. (Isaiah 40:1-2, NIV)

Break forth together into singing,
you waste places of Jerusalem,
for the LORD has comforted his people;
he has redeemed Jerusalem. (Isaiah 52:9)

The Messiah Comes

The baptism of Jesus during the ministry of John the Baptist marks the beginning of Jesus' Messianic ministry (Matthew 3:13-17, Mark 1:9-11, Luke 3:21-22, John 1:31-34).

John the Baptist came to baptize for two purposes. The first was to prepare the people for the Messiah. The second was to present the Messiah to the people (John 1:31). One was preparation, the other was presentation. Jesus did not submit to baptism to repent of sin. He submitted to baptism to present himself publicly as the Messiah.

During his baptism, Jesus' identity as the Messiah was confirmed by God in heaven in two ways based on Psalm 2.

Psalm 2 is considered to be one of the most Messianic psalms in the Old Testament. It speaks of a king of Israel, a *Māshiach* anointed by God, who will rule the nations for God as a viceroy, and who stood in relation to God in heaven as a son would to a father. It reads in full—

Why do the nations rage
and the peoples plot in vain?
2 The kings of the earth set themselves,
and the rulers take counsel together,
against the LORD and against his Anointed, saying,

3 "Let us burst their bonds apart
and cast away their cords from us."
4 He who sits in the heavens laughs;
the Lord holds them in derision.
5 Then he will speak to them in his wrath,
and terrify them in his fury, saying,
6 "As for me, I have set my King
on Zion, my holy hill."
7 I will tell of the decree:
The LORD said to me, "You are my Son;
today I have begotten you.
8 Ask of me, and I will make the nations your heritage,
and the ends of the earth your possession.
9 You shall break them with a rod of iron
and dash them in pieces like a potter's vessel."
10 Now therefore, O kings, be wise;
be warned, O rulers of the earth.
11 Serve the LORD with fear,
and rejoice with trembling.
12 Kiss the Son,
lest he be angry, and you perish in the way,
for his wrath is quickly kindled.
Blessed are all who take refuge in him.

When Jesus was baptized, his identity as the Messiah was confirmed by two things that happened during his baptism. First, a voice was heard from heaven that identified Jesus as the Messiah, King and Servant. It said—

"This is my beloved Son, with whom I am well pleased."
(Matthew 3:17)

This is an allusion to and combination of both Psalm 2:7 (the Messiah King) as well as Isaiah 42:1 (the Servant)—

I will tell of the decree:
The LORD said to me, "You are my Son;
today I have begotten you. (Psalm 2:7)

Behold my servant, whom I uphold,

> *my chosen, in whom my soul delights;*
> *I have put my Spirit upon him;*
> *he will bring forth justice to the nations. (Isaiah 42:1)*

Secondly, during the baptism of Jesus, God in heaven anointed Jesus with the Spirit of God in the form of a dove as a sign that he was the Messiah, just as Psalm 2 speaks of the Messiah as being the 'Anointed' of the LORD—

> *And when Jesus was baptized, immediately he went up from the water,*
> *and behold, the heavens were opened to him, and he saw the Spirit of*
> *God descending like a dove and coming to rest on him. (Matthew 3:16)*

> *The kings of the earth set themselves,*
> *and the rulers take counsel together,*
> *against the LORD and against his Anointed. (Psalm 2:2)*

The baptism of Jesus, with these two signs from heaven, based on Psalm 2, confirmed that he was the Messiah. That is why later, when the chief priests and elders challenged Jesus to say by what authority he was doing his ministry, he replied simply—

> *The baptism of John, from where did it come?*
> *From heaven or from man?" (Matthew 21:25)*

Jesus answered as he did not only to stymie his opponents with a question they could not answer, but also because his baptism *is* the proof of his authority as the Messiah (Matthew 21:23-26). He is the Messiah King of Psalm 2.

The Messianic Age Begins

After Jesus' baptism, the Spirit of God drove him into the desert to be tempted by Satan. Unlike Israel, which had failed its test in the wilderness, Jesus succeeded, proving that he was the 'new Israel'—the head of the Messianic kingdom.

Immediately afterwards, he returns to Galilee and announces that the long-waited kingdom of God was finally at hand—

> *The time is fulfilled, and the kingdom of God is at hand;*
> *repent and believe in the gospel. (Mark 1:15)*

Following this announcement, the opening chapters of the Gospel of Mark record an outpouring of healings and exorcisms that happened at the beginning of Jesus' ministry. This is remarkable because in all of the Old Testament there are just a few instances of healings and exorcisms. Mark purposefully opens his Gospel with an outpouring of healings and exorcisms to demonstrate that the Messianic age had truly arrived in the person of Jesus. God was breaking into Satan's realm through Christ to redeem humanity. The 'present age' (Hebrew: *'olam hazeh*), marked by demonic activity, sickness and evil was giving way to the Messianic Era, known as the 'age to come' (Hebrew: *'olam haba*).

The Gospel of John also speaks of Jesus' displays of power as the Messiah in a similar yet slightly different way. It contains seven 'sign-miracles' (Greek: *semeia*): the changing of the water into wine, the healing of the nobleman's son, the healing at Bethesda, the feeding of the 5,000, the walking on water, the healing of the man born blind and the raising of Lazarus from the dead.

A *semeia* miracle is more than a display of power; it is a sign miracle meant to reveal an identity—in this case, the identity of Jesus as the Messiah.

There appears to have been a popular expectation, as reflected in the extra-biblical source of 2 Baruch 29:5-8, that when the Messiah came he would restore the giving of manna from heaven and cause the land to yield an overwhelming abundance of grapes. This may be why, when Jesus fed the 5,000 from a few loaves and fishes, it was seen as a sign that pointed to his identity as the manna-giving Messiah (Exodus 16, John 6:30-40). And when Jesus changed the water into wine, it was understood to be another sign miracle which identified him as the promised Messiah.

Jesus is the Kingdom-in-Person

Mark's Gospel begins by emphasizing that the Messianic Age had arrived. Not only did Jesus announce that "the kingdom of God is at hand," but Mark then depicts the kingdom as breaking into Satan's realm through Jesus' miracles and exorcisms.

Many expected that when the kingdom came, it would be an all-powerful version of the nation of Israel. But in Luke 17:21, Jesus further defines the nature of this kingdom when he answers a question from the Pharisees about its coming. Jesus tells them—

For behold, the kingdom of God is in the midst of you.

Here, he does not identify the coming kingdom as being a supranational Israel. Nor does he say that the kingdom was *within* them, as some mistakenly translate this verse, since Jesus says elsewhere that the Pharisees, to whom he was speaking, were far from the kingdom (Matthew 23:13). Rather, Jesus is saying that the kingdom was within their midst, standing right in front of them. Jesus the Messiah was claiming to be the '*kingdom-in-person.*'

The context of the Old Testament helps us to better understand the import of what Jesus is claiming. The Old Testament assumes that God, being the Creator, is sovereign over all nations: "The LORD has established his throne in the heavens, and his kingdom rules over all" (Psalm 103:19). Because the kingdom of God was much bigger than Israel, Jesus did not characterize the coming kingdom as being an all-powerful version of Israel.

Instead, Jesus identifies the kingdom with himself. This is an astonishing claim since the expectation was that the Messiah would be a human agent who acts with God's authority as God's viceroy on earth. But here, in asserting that he is the kingdom-in-person, Jesus is saying he is more than a human agent.

This is why the Gospels freely included Jesus in the unique identity of God in heaven by recording how he forgave sins, cast out demons, raised the dead, calmed a storm and commissioned the apostles to make disciples of the nations. It is also why Jesus claimed pre-existence (John 8:58) and said that "I and the Father are one" (John 10:30). Even more, the New Testament openly sees a unity between the Creator and the Redeemer. Paul writes of Christ, "For by him all things were created … all things were created through him and for him" and "in him all things hold together" (Colossians 1:16-17). And John writes not only that the world was created by the Word but it is also being redeemed by the Word made flesh (John 1:1-3, 14).

And this also explains why Jesus' death as the Messiah has the atoning power to forgive sin and to redeem the nations from the power of the devil. It is because in Christ God Himself is the Suffering Servant who redeems us from sin, as Isaiah foresaw (Isaiah 52:13-53:12, Hebrews 2:14-15; also, notice the parallels between the Redeemer of Isaiah 59:20-21 with Jesus in Acts 2:38-39). Apart from the Cross, we could never understand this essential attribute of God.

Since Christ is the *kingdom-in-person*, his kingdom is unlike the kingdoms of this world (John 18:36). One enters it by having the humility of a child. One becomes great in it by living a life of service rather than hungering for power (Matthew 18:1-4). One continues in it by learning "to observe all that I have commanded you" (Matthew 28:20). One shares in its joy by learning to trust in the providential care of our heavenly Father. We are told to "Seek first the kingdom of God and his righteousness" (Matthew 6:33). As we do so, our Messiah King instills in us a deep wisdom that makes our lives increasingly whole.

To confess that Jesus is the Messiah, then, means to acknowledge that:

(1) He has the authority to rule the nations (Psalm 2, Matthew 28:18-20, Romans 10:9).

(2) Through him, the reign of God is breaking into the world.

(3) His atoning sacrifice is sufficient to redeem the sin of people from all nations (Luke 24:46-47, 1 John 2:2).

(4) His wisdom teaches us how to live under God's reign.

The Church and Its Mission

Luke tells us that, after Jesus rose from the dead, he appeared to the apostles over forty days and taught them about the kingdom of God (Acts 1:3). During that instruction, they asked him, "Lord, will you at this time restore the kingdom to Israel?" (1:6).

Apparently they thought, as many did at that time, that there would be a sharp transition from the 'present age' (*'olam hazeh*), to the 'age to come,' (*'olam haba*) when the Messiah would fully reign. They also seemed to have identified the kingdom of God with a supranational Israel.

In his reply, Jesus says—

> "It is not for you to know times or seasons that the Father has fixed by his own authority. 8 But you will receive power when the Holy Spirit has come upon you, and you will be my witnesses in Jerusalem and in all Judea and Samaria, and to the end of the earth." (Acts 1:7-8)

In saying this, Jesus reshapes their understanding of the two ages. There will be no sharp transition between the 'present age' and the 'age to come.' The 'age to come' has already begun, even while the 'present age' is still continuing. Even though the Church lives in the present age, it is called to share in the in-breaking of the age to come by bearing witness to Christ. This means it will continue to experience evil and sorrow, sickness and death, even while also tasting of the "powers of the age to come" (Hebrews 6:5).

The Church's mission is to fulfill the Great Commission—

> And Jesus came and said to them, "All authority in heaven and on earth has been given to me. 19 Go therefore and make disciples of all nations, baptizing them in the name of the Father and of the Son and of the Holy Spirit, 20 teaching them to observe all that I have commanded you. And behold, I am with you always, to the end of the age." (Matthew 28:18-20)

Here, the phrase 'I am with you' is very interesting. In the Greek, 'I am' is often phrased as *ego eimi*. But here, *ego eimi* is divided, with the words—'with you'—nestled in-between. And so it reads: "*ego*—'*with you*'—*eimi.*" It is a subtle emphasis on Jesus' promise to be with us as we go and make disciples of the nations.

Jesus goes with us through the agency of the Holy Spirit. This is something that Luke, in particular, emphasizes in *Acts*, especially in the story of Pentecost (Acts 1-2). Jesus being the Messiah, the 'Anointed One' upon whom the Spirit of God rests (Psalm 2, Isaiah 11:1-2), pours out the Spirit on the Church to empower it to disciple the nations. Peter explains—

> Being therefore exalted at the right hand of God, and having received from the Father the promise of the Holy Spirit, he has poured out this that you yourselves are seeing and hearing. (Acts 2:33)

Acts recounts the signs and wonders and conviction of sin that occurred as the Messiah poured out the Spirit, confirming the message which the apostles preached.

With the outpouring of the Holy Spirit on the disciples on Pentecost, the Church immediately began its task of bearing witness to the nations—affirming that the kingdom of God is meant for all peoples, whoever accepts God as their king.

But while Jesus used the word *kingdom* to describe the Messianic age, the Church preferred to speak about Jesus as *Lord*, since he is the kingdom-in-person. In doing so, the Church boldly saw Jesus as sharing in the identity of God in heaven. For instance, the word *'Lord'* (Greek: *kurios*) is used over 6000 times for God in the Septuagint, the Greek version of the Old Testament. The writers of the New Testament were well aware of this when they applied the same word to Jesus. Most notable is the phrase, "Jesus is Lord," which appears to have been the earliest confession of the Church (Romans 10:9, 1 Corinthians 12:3).

Also notable is 1 Corinthians 8:6, which modifies the *Shema*, the Jewish confession of faith, to include Jesus. The Shema reads—

> *Hear, O Israel: The LORD our God, the LORD is one (Deuteronomy 6:4).*

Paul modified this to include Jesus in the identity of God—

> *There is one God, the Father, from whom are all things and for whom we exist, and one Lord, Jesus Christ, through whom are all things and through whom we exist. (1 Corinthians 8:6)*

Recognizing the Lordship of Christ, and knowing that his kingdom was to include peoples from all nations, the early disciples responded to Jesus' Great Commission to evangelize the nations. Quickly, house churches were formed, often in a hostile climate. This opposition, and the possibility of oppression and persecution, is reflected in many parts of the New Testament, such as *Acts, 1 and 2 Thessalonians, Hebrews, 1 Peter* and *Revelation*.

Other parts of the New Testament give evidence to the cultural oppression that weighed against the church. Just as the

Church sought to change the world for God, so also the world sought to undermine the Church. There was the ever-present danger of heresy, as *Colossians, 1 Timothy, 2 Peter, 1 John, Jude* and *Revelation 2-3* give witness. Basic Christian ethics and values were also at risk of erosion, especially for immature believers, as *1 and 2 Corinthians* demonstrate. Still, despite all, the Church continued to bear witness and to grow in the Roman world.

Another Purpose of the Church

Besides being a witness for God, another purpose of the Church is to be one people for God. This is a major theme of the New Testament which is often overlooked. *Acts* and Paul's letters to the *Galatians* and *Ephesians* document the intense controversy surrounding the integration of Gentiles into a Church that was predominately Jewish at the time.

Of all the early leaders of the Church, only Paul had the penetrating theological insight necessary to guide the Church through those rough waters. *Ephesians*, in particular, is a masterpiece of insight about how Christ is calling the nations to be one people for God. Paul wrote, for instance, in Ephesians 2:11-16 —

> *Therefore remember that at one time you Gentiles in the flesh, called "the uncircumcision" by what is called the circumcision, which is made in the flesh by hands— 12 remember that you were at that time separated from Christ, alienated from the commonwealth of Israel and strangers to the covenants of promise, having no hope and without God in the world. 13 But now in Christ Jesus you who once were far off have been brought near by the blood of Christ. 14 For he himself is our peace, who has made us both one and has broken down in his flesh the dividing wall of hostility 15 by abolishing the law of commandments expressed in ordinances, that he might create in himself one new man in place of the two, so making peace, 16 and might reconcile us both to God in one body through the cross, thereby killing the hostility.*

The inclusion of the Gentiles in the kingdom of God had been part of God's plan of redemption all along. We can see it in God's promise to Abraham that "in you all the families of the earth shall be blessed" (Genesis 12:3). Isaiah also prophesied that the nations would be included in the messianic kingdom (Isaiah 2:2-4, 11:9, 42:1-9, 49:5-6, 56:3-7, 60:1-14). But this insight had been neglected, so God revealed this truth anew to Paul, causing him to write as if it was a mystery finally unveiled. As Paul writes in Ephesians 3:6—

> *This mystery is that the Gentiles are fellow heirs, members of the same body, and partakers of the promise in Christ Jesus through the gospel.*

Paul prays for the Ephesians to be able to grasp God's master plan of redemption, which now included the Gentiles (Ephesians 3:14-21). He also interprets his own apostleship as playing a key role in its fulfillment (Ephesians 3:1-13, 6:19; see also Romans 16:25-26, Ephesians 1:9-12, Colossians 1:25-27).

Paul's letter to the *Romans* is another masterpiece of deep theological thinking addressing the issue of how the Church can be one people for God. It is a theological explanation of how both Jew and Gentile are included in God's salvation.

Romans appears designed to answer three main questions pertaining to this issue—

1) How can Gentiles be included in God's plan of salvation? (Romans 1-2; 3:9-8:39)

2) Does God still have a special relationship with the Jews? (3:1-8, chapters 9-11)

3) What does the redefined people of God look like, Jew and Gentile? (chapters 12-15)

Accordingly, the key verse for Romans is Romans 1:16-17. It teaches not only that we are saved by faith in Christ, but also that God is making us into one people in Christ—

For I am not ashamed of the gospel, for it is the power of God for salvation to everyone who believes, to the Jew first and also to the Greek. 17 For in it the righteousness of God is revealed from faith for faith, as it is written, "The righteous shall live by faith."

The Final Inheritance

The New Testament uses the phrase *'eternal life'* to refer to life that comes from God and belongs to the age to come. And so, Paul writes that we were once "dead in the trespasses and sins," but God has "made us alive together with Christ" and "raised us up with him and seated us with him in the heavenly places in Christ Jesus" (Ephesians 2:1, 5, 6). For the believer, eternal life has already begun. The believer already shares in the eternal inheritance, but not fully so.

The sign that this is true for believers is the indwelling presence of the Holy Spirit within them. The Spirit, "is the guarantee of our inheritance until we acquire possession of it" (Ephesians 1:14). Here, the Greek word for *'guarantee'* is *'arabon,'* which signifies a deposit or a down payment of all that is promised. Every experience the believer has of the Holy Spirit is a confirmation of the full inheritance which awaits us.

The Church evangelized the Roman world with the expectation that, at any moment, the 'present age' could suddenly end and the messianic 'age to come' would fully arrive. When that Day comes, the redeemed will fully receive their final inheritance. Paul writes of the sudden coming of that Day as an event when—

… the Lord Jesus is revealed from heaven with his mighty angels in flaming fire, inflicting vengeance on those who do not know God and on those who do not obey the gospel of our Lord Jesus. (2 Thessalonians 1:7-8)

For now, the believer lives 'betwixt the times.' We experience decay and suffering and frustration in this world, even as we wait for our full inheritance, our glorification—

> *18 For I consider that the sufferings of this present time are not worth comparing with the glory that is to be revealed to us. ... 21 the creation itself will be set free from its bondage to corruption and obtain the freedom of the glory of the children of God. 22 For we know that the whole creation has been groaning together in the pains of childbirth until now. 23 And not only the creation, but we ourselves, who have the firstfruits of the Spirit, groan inwardly as we wait eagerly for adoption as sons, the redemption of our bodies. (Romans 8:18, 21-23)*

The culmination of God's plan of salvation is when the Messiah finishes his work as God's viceroy on earth and delivers the kingdom to God in heaven—

> *24 Then comes the end, when he delivers the kingdom to God the Father after destroying every rule and every authority and power. 25 For he must reign until he has put all his enemies under his feet. 26 The last enemy to be destroyed is death. (1 Corinthians 15:24-26)*

A final picture that we are given of our inheritance in Christ comes from the last chapters of *Revelation*. Using representational language to describe the indescribable, it likens our eternal existence to a city built of purified gold and precious jewels, where God dwells, and which possesses the tree of life (Revelation 21-22). It is a home without tears, decay or death— a return to Eden where a redeemed humanity has been welcomed to live once more, where the redemptive promises of God—the first made in the Garden, a second announced to Abraham and a third given to David—are finally and fully reached.

Summary of the Book

We began this book by saying that if people today no longer believe that there are any grand explanations to life that you or I can create, then the only true metanarrative would have to come from God—the ground of our being. We have tried to show the evidence for the existence of this metanarrative in the Bible. The biblical metanarrative is the story of God making himself known to us as our Creator, Provider and Redeemer. God truly loves us and wants to know us and be known by us.

God revealed himself to the world by walking with a chosen people for many centuries. It was done this way, apparently, because we have been entrusted with a role in making God known to the world.

With each of the major events, or epochs, in God's relationship with his people, certain aspects of God's character were emphasized or made known—

Major Event:	God As:
Creation	Creator
The Fall	Judge
Call of Abraham	Covenant-Maker
Exodus	Redeemer
Israel as a Nation	King
Israel in Exile	The Holy One
The Restoration	The Merciful One
Fulfillment	The Suffering Servant

The self-revelation of God reached a culmination in the person of the Messiah, who is the Promised Redeemer. The mystery of his atoning death as the Suffering Servant for the sins of the nations can only be understood if it is seen as the climax of the self-revelation of God to the world. In the Messiah—his life, atoning death and resurrection—we come to know God as fully as we can. King Messiah is the Way back to the Garden, our home and inheritance.

Knowing this to be true, let us boldly believe and proclaim the good news—"the kingdom of God is at hand!"

9 Teaching the Biblical Metanarrative

When we present the Gospel to someone who does not understand its biblical context, it sounds unintelligible to them. One day, as a youthful evangelist, I told someone, "Jesus can save you!" Their reply was a puzzled look and the question, "Save me from what?"

The biblical context of the Gospel gives meaning to the message. D. A. Carson writes, "The good news of Jesus is virtually incoherent unless it is squarely set into a biblical worldview" (*The Gagging of God*, 1996, pg. 502). As someone has said, it is like walking in on a movie half-way and trying to figure out what's going on. What we may interpret as disinterest or rejection on the part of our listeners might simply be bewilderment at what we're talking about. This is why teaching people the biblical metanarrative is an important first step in evangelism today.

The creation account in Genesis is a good place to start since it sets the foundation of the entire biblical worldview. Unfortunately, the arguments that we can have over the creation account, such as how old the earth is, can divert us from hearing what it is saying about the four important worldview questions—

Where did I come from?
What is the meaning of life?
How do I define right from wrong?
What happens to me when I die?

When people begin thinking biblically about these questions, a biblical worldview begins to be established in their minds.

We then can build on this foundation by focusing on the key stories in the Bible which mark the epochal events in the history of salvation. But it is not enough simply to learn the stories; one must also see how the stories connect to the plan and the purpose of God in the Bible as a whole. Doing so gives the learner a sense of the biblical metanarrative.

The documentary video, *Ee-Taow!,* illustrates the effectiveness of teaching the Gospel in this way. The video, produced by *New Tribes Mission*, concerns a village in Papua New Guinea which had never heard of the Gospel. Teaching daily, the missionaries first presented the creation account and then other key stories from the Bible so their listeners could develop a biblical worldview and understand the flow of the biblical metanarrative. Only after six months of this groundwork did the missionaries present the story of Christ. The Gospel immediately made sense to the villagers and most of them responded to it. The video has been posted on *YouTube.*

Today, there is an increasing interest in teaching the biblical metanarrative:

In *mission work,* many are now reporting the value of chronological Bible story-telling as an indispensible part of the process of evangelism, similar to what was demonstrated in *Ee-Taow!*

In *Christian education,* a number of excellent curriculums are now available which teach the 'Big Story' of the Bible. Even *New Tribes Mission* has developed a curriculum for use in postmodern, developed countries. It is based on their experience in Papua New Guinea.

In *preaching,* there is a new emphasis on relating texts to the greater redemptive context of the Bible and not just to the immediate historical context. Doing so helps a congregation to develop a sense of the Bible as a whole.

People are also finding *small group ministries* to be a perfect venue for teaching the biblical metanarrative. Inductive Bible studies, especially, allow people to ask questions and process information at their own pace. A small group, for instance, could study Genesis slowly and inductively over six months—giving people time to develop a biblical worldview and to discover the existence of the biblical metanarrative in the text.

The reader is also invited to use present book as a basis for discussion in small groups.

10 For Further Reading

Many excellent resources are available for studying the biblical metanarrative at a more advanced level. Among the following examples, those with an asterisk are especially recommended.

Biblical Theologies

Goldsworthy, Graeme. *According to Plan: The Unfolding Revelation of God in the Bible* (2002).

Hamilton, James M. Jr. *God's Glory in Salvation through Judgment: A Biblical Theology* (2010).

Kaiser, Walter C. Jr. *The Promise-Plan of God: A Biblical Theology of the Old and New Testaments* (2008). *

Rosner, Brian S. and T. Desmond Alexander. *New Dictionary of Biblical Theology: Exploring the Unity & Diversity of Scripture* (2000). *

VanGemeren, Willem. *The Progress of Redemption: The Story of Salvation from Creation to the New Jerusalem* (1996).

Thematic Approaches

Bauckham, Richard. *God Crucified: Monotheism and Christology in the New Testament* (1998).

Bright, John. *The Kingdom of God* (1953).

Bruce, F. F. *The New Testament Development of Old Testament Themes* (1968).

Clowney, Edmund P. *The Unfolding Mystery: Discovering Christ in the Old Testament* (1988; 2nd ed., 2013).

Wright, Christopher J. H. *The Mission of God: Unlocking the Bible's Grand Narrative* (2006).

Made in the USA
Middletown, DE
20 September 2023

38866144R00057